The Woodlands

The

Texas A&M UNIVERSITY PRESS
COLLEGE STATION

Woodlands

New Community Development, 1964–1983

George T. Morgan, Jr.
and
John O. King

Library of Congress Cataloging-in-Publication Data

Morgan, George T. (George Thomas), 1931–
    The Woodlands : new community development, 1964–1983.

    Bibliography: p.
    Includes index.
    1. Woodlands (Tex.) – History. 2. New towns – Texas –
Woodlands – History. I. King, John O. II. Title.
HT169.57.U62W665 1987   307.7′68′09764141   86-23081
ISBN 0-89096-306-1

FOR THE MEMORY OF
George T. Morgan, Sr.
AND
Mary Elizabeth King
AND FOR
Gladys A. Morgan

Contents

Illustrations

Preface

This study is an assessment of both the dreams and the realities of new-community development as seen in the early history of The Woodlands, Texas.

There is much to be celebrated in the as yet unfinished story of the lone viable new town created under the aegis of federal legislation. There is also more than a little to be mourned. The Woodlands stands on the one hand as a monument to a grand experiment wrought by the many men and women who sought to unite American society behind their vision of a more nearly perfect everyday environment for urban dwellers. The early history of The Woodlands serves on the other hand as a reminder of a democratic society's often fatal habit of failing to sustain long-range programs despite periodic fluctuations in the economic index, the ebb and flow of social tensions, and the rise and fall of individual political fortunes.

The making of this book depended on the talents and resources of many people. The officers and staff of Mitchell Energy and Development Corporation were unfailing in helping us find long-forgotten and sometimes misplaced documents and in their candid responses to our endless probing, regardless of the delicacy of the subject. We are particularly grateful to George P. Mitchell; Edward P. Lee, Jr.; J. Leonard Rogers; Joel Deretchin; Richard P. Browne; Randall Woods; Charles Lively; Coulson Tough; David Bumgardner; Paul W. Wommack; and Robinson G. Lapp for their uninhibited recollections of the roles played by themselves and others in the development of The Woodlands. Donald R. Gebert and Charles Kelly provided equally provocative commentaries which helped us sharpen our perspective. The staff of *The Woodlands Villager* opened the dusty bins holding discarded issues, joined in the hunt for missing early copies, and graciously ignored necessary detours around the researcher's piled treasure. Special credit must also go to Mel DuPaix, who provided statistical material, and to Clifford Roe, whose photographer's skills proved indispensable in the preparation of illustrations, all of which appear courtesy of the Mitchell Energy and Development Corporation.

We are also indebted to our typist, Marta Remington Zulauf, and especially to our colleague, Gerald J. Goodwin, whose critical reading of the manuscript and editorial suggestions improved both interpretation and narrative. Finally, no words can express our gratitude to Joseph Kutchin and Charles Simpson for their unwavering support, counsel, and friendship. They share responsibility with the authors for whatever merit the book possesses and none for its shortcomings.

The Woodlands

1. Prologue

Visitors to The Woodlands, Texas, leave Interstate 45 approximately ten miles south of Conroe and twenty-seven miles north of downtown Houston. Once off the busy highway and beyond the unsightly billboards, neon signs, junkyards, and fast-food stores, they enter a serene and sylvan world quite unlike the one they just left. Driving along a broad, tree-lined boulevard uncluttered with utility poles and wires, they spot a lake through the foliage and here and there catch a glimpse of rooftops or a glass-sided office building, all barely discernible amid a panoply of pine and oak trees.

Veteran city dwellers, the visitors watch for the usual nondescript street signs perched atop slender poles at whatever angle uninterested workmen or prankish children chose to leave them. They search in vain. There are no such markers in The Woodlands; instead, when finally they sight one, it is constructed of natural wood and set unobtrusively low to the ground so as to blend into the sylvan background.

Spotting a sign marked "Information Center," the visitors turn into a wooded cul-de-sac and stop in front of a building which also complements, and is complemented by, its forest setting. Inside they are greeted by a hostess, who escorts them, along with other guests, into a screening room to view a multimedia presentation called *Time and Space*. A well-done advertising piece, the film presents the viewers with scenes depicting the unspoiled, natural beauty of The Woodlands and the relaxed, leisurely lives enjoyed by its residents at work and at play. The film accurately portrays the natural environment of The Woodlands and the minimal impact on it of man's presence. In that sense also it reflects the vision of the founder of The Woodlands, George P. Mitchell.

Biographical sketches of Mitchell invariably mention that he does not conform to the stereotyped public image of a Texas oilman. He is not a bulky, bullnecked, leathery character, feisty, independent, and of single-minded purpose and outlook. In his mid-sixties, George Mitchell is trim, physically fit through a long devotion to tennis, articulate, and decidedly catholic in his thinking and interests. His active role as a leader of the American petroleum industry is extremely time-consuming, but his interests also include such diversified subjects as urban planning, historical restoration of his native Galveston, and the sponsorship of internationally acclaimed conferences on global environmental, population, and natural-resource problems.[1]

Mitchell's heritage is also rather remote from Texas. He is the youngest son of Greek immigrant parents. His father, at the age of twenty, came to this country in 1903 from southern Greece and worked for several years as a laborer, building western railroads. When a gang foreman threatened to fire him because of his unwieldy name, Sava Paraskivopoulis, he shortened it to Mike Mitchell—the gang boss's name.

Like many other immigrants, Mike Mitchell prospered in America. In 1905 he settled in Houston and opened a cleaning and pressing shop. He married in 1910, and later, in 1911, he moved his family to Galveston and opened another dry-cleaning business. He bought a parcel of real estate in a Galveston that was still recovering from the disastrous hurricane of a decade before and made a meager living for his family as owner of a small cleaning and pressing shop. He struggled to help his three sons and a daughter to attend universities, although he had never been in school a day in his life.

Son George was born in Galveston in 1919. He attended local elementary schools and graduated from Ball High School. He then enrolled in Texas A&M, where he graduated first in his class with a hard-earned degree in petroleum engineering with emphasis on geology. Of the five hundred students who started this major with Mitchell, only fifty graduated in his class.

1. The following materials were used in compiling Mitchell's biographical data: "George P. Mitchell: Biographical Sketch," Communications Office, Mitchell Energy & Development Corporation; "Nobody's Laughing Now," Forbes Magazine 127 (March 2, 1981): 84–88; Tom Curtis, "Masterbuilder—George Mitchell Is No Ordinary Oilman," Sky, September, 1977, pp. 41, 78; "A Texas Oilman Takes on America's Urban Congestion," Boston Sunday Globe, November 16, 1975; "Mitchell Wants Woodlands to Ease Urban Ills," Houston Chronicle, October 23, 1977.

Aerial view, The Woodlands, 1986.

Although he paid most of his college expenses by working at such prosaic tasks as waiting tables, he later found a more ingenious solution to the usual problem of money shortage. During his junior year he earned about $150 a month selling gold-embossed stationery, as he later reminisced, "to lovesick freshmen who wanted to impress their sweethearts."[2] And it was not all work and classes at A&M: Mitchell, an excellent tennis player since his high school days, captained and played on the A&M varsity team.

After he graduated from college in 1940 the American Oil Company (Amoco) employed him as a $126-a-month geologist to prospect for oil in Louisiana. Then came Pearl Harbor. The holder of an ROTC

2. *Houston Chronicle,* October 23, 1977.

commission gained at Texas A&M, Mitchell soon received a call to active duty as a second lieutenant in the Army Corps of Engineers and spent the war years supervising the construction of military facilities in the Gulf Coast area. When he was mustered out in 1946, he had risen to the rank of major.

Mitchell decided not to return to Amoco after the war. He began as a geological consultant and later worked with a brother and another partner. This group often recruited a syndicate of twenty to thirty people to underwrite drilling costs. Mitchell then supplied his geological expertise on how and where to drill. If a productive well came in, Mitchell and his firm shared in the profits. His advice proved sound more often than not. Consequently, the firm prospered and expanded through the years by what he has styled as "geometric dimensions" into the company that ultimately became Mitchell Energy and Development Corporation.[3]

Today the company is one of the country's major independent petroleum producers with assets of more than $2 billion and is among the firms on the *Fortune* 500 list. Through its Exploration and Production Division, Mitchell Energy and Development Corporation has interests in more than twenty-five hundred productive wells and holds leases on approximately 3.9 million acres in twenty-five states and Canada. Its Transmission and Processing Division owns or has interest in over thirty-eight hundred miles of gas-gathering and transmission pipelines mainly in Texas, but with gas-pipeline properties also in Louisiana, Pennsylvania, and Wyoming. This division also owns fifty-seven gas-processing plants, most of which are operated in conjunction with its pipeline properties.[4]

The Woodlands project is the most visible undertaking in Mitchell Energy and Development Corporation's Real Estate Division. Its revenues account for the vast majority of the division's gross revenues. But various other properties managed by the division should also be noted: Magnolia Country, which includes Clear Creek Forest, West Magnolia Forest, and Lake Creek Forest subdivisions, is a residential development in Montgomery, Waller, and Grimes counties. Pelican Island, an industrial site, is on the ship channel at Galveston Island, Texas. Pirates' Beach, Pirates' Cove, and Indian Beach subdivisions on the west end of Galveston Island are Mitchell's ventures into residential-recreational prop-

3. Ibid.

4. Mitchell Energy and Development Corporation, First Quarter Report, April 30, 1982; Mitchell Energy and Development Corporation, Annual Report, Year Ended January 31, 1983. The following review of the company's operations are from this source.

erty. Two other such developments are Cape Royale, at Lake Livingston, Texas, and Point Venture, at Lake Travis, Texas. The company also owns for future development substantial acreage between Buttermilk Mountain and Snowmass, near Alpine, Colorado. In recent years Mitchell Energy and Development Corporation has held a total of sixty thousand or more acres of real estate, most of them within a fifty-mile radius of Houston.

Mitchell's career has its symbolic qualities. He is an excellent example of the "new breed" of Texas oilman who entered the industry in the post–World War II years—young, professionally trained, talented in corporate administration and personnel management, versatile, and in some areas visionary. These qualities plus a sense of social responsibility led Mitchell into an ambitious project of urban planning and development.

As a lifelong resident of the Houston-Galveston metropolitan region Mitchell participated actively in its development and prospered with his native area. Yet events of the 1960s which punctuated the dangers to society posed by city slums and helter-skelter urban growth concerned him. Throughout the country the flight of the more affluent to the suburbs often reduced the inner city to a decaying section usually inhabited by lower-income minorities. Reduced tax revenues brought diminished municipal services, particularly educational and social services. Poor educational opportunities further trapped inner-city residents in unemployment, poverty, and crime. The general national unrest of the 1960s, additionally agitated by the Vietnam War and the civil-rights movement, instigated widespread urban protests and, at times, violence.

Mitchell knew both as an alert businessman and as an informed citizen that his own Houston-Galveston area suffered from the same ills that plagued other metropolitan areas. Unlike other equally aware persons, he resolved to seek a better approach to urban development. As the head of a diversified energy company with significant real estate ventures, he had some practical experience. He read widely on the subject and noted that typical patterns of inner-city decay had begun to appear in downtown Houston. He further noticed that the flight of affluent whites to Houston suburbs often brought neither order nor aesthetics to the environment of those areas. West Houston's Memorial area, where he resided, undoubtedly developed as an "upper-end" community, but a beautiful wooded section had become the victim of "helter-skelter, fragmented development . . . that now has real problems." The failure to use the natural setting to its fullest extent brought further questions and challenges. He asked, "If you were going to take   7

Memorial and wipe it all out and do it all over again, how would you do it better?"[5]

Certain of Mitchell's ideas began to take shape as he further thought about the urban problems of the late 1960s. At this point his ideas lacked focus, but their substance convinced him of the need to explore further. In essence he conceived of a "totally" new community within the Houston metropolitan area with an eventual population of about 180,000. This planned community would offer a variety of low-to-high-income housing and achieve a significant degree of racial and economic integration. This process would be accepted because of superior environmental, cultural, educational, and recreational facilities. Above all, through proper planning and utilization of the community's natural attributes, it could be a pleasant, healthy, and harmonious place to live. The problems of the inner city—pollution, traffic, congestion, noise, and general urban blight—could be alleviated. Mitchell thought that his ideas, without being excessively utopian, presented an excellent chance to improve on mankind's urban environment.

Further, he reasoned, the community need not complicate the ills of the inner city. It would help in their solution since the community eventually would be incorporated into the metropolis. It could thus furnish additional tax revenues to support and upgrade municipal services, particularly in its welcome support of the inner city's public school system. Residents of the inner city might be lured to the new community, but the new community would not be parasitic. Its residents— their taxes, their cultural and educational attainments—would contribute to the betterment and support of the city. Yet Mitchell was realistic. This was not a quick solution to urban ills but necessitated a long-range commitment that might take a generation or more to fulfill.[6]

Another very practical problem had to be faced. Granted that his ideas had substance and validity, how was the new community to be financed? The answer assumed the union of altruistic motivation and entrepreneurial spirit. The success of the project in achieving its theoretical goals ensured a successful business venture. As Mitchell put it, "I had an interest in figuring out how we do it and do it as an economic venture that made sense profit-wise."[7]

The project also made sense to Mitchell as the chief executive of a petroleum corporation. A successful real estate operation could contribute a high degree of stability to offset the volatility of oil-and-gas

5. Interview with George P. Mitchell, October 16, 1979.
6. Ibid.
7. Ibid.

operations. For fifteen years Mitchell had warned that the country faced an impending energy crisis. This crisis would arise from a restrictive public policy inhibiting domestic petroleum production and the resulting reliance on imported oil, particularly from the politically uncertain Middle East. The new community made sense as a "vehicle that we could get into with a high leverage . . . [to] survive a serious problem of oil and gas during those years."[8]

But could private sources effectively finance a project of the size and scope that Mitchell visualized? Initially he thought that it could be done, though preliminary estimates soon indicated substantial problems involving the uncertain economic conditions of the period. It was estimated that in its initial phases the project required about $7 million a year for land purchases and development costs. Interest rates of that time, under increasing inflationary pressures, were edging into the 10 percent range. Such a debt-service burden would, of course, delay completion of the project and cycle substantial increases into the project's cost.

Solutions to the problem of financing ultimately came through the federal government's apparent commitment to enhancing the quality of urban life with the passage of the new-community acts of 1968 and 1970. The act of 1970, with its loan guarantees of up to $50 million for a project, offered Mitchell a "partnership" with the government with substantial inducements for his participation. The project could be funded immediately, without a prolonged development period, and eventually completed at a substantially lower cost. Such a relationship, of course, meant that the developer and the government's administrative authority, the Department of Housing and Urban Development (HUD), would be compelled to share substantial elements of executive policy and decision making. Mitchell's eventual decision to enter such a partnership was a fateful one which would have far-reaching effects on his company and his nascent project.

8. Ibid.

2. New Towns and Old Ideas

Americans, perhaps because of their frontier heritage, have a special attachment to the pastoral, both symbolic and actual. Their historical identification with the bucolic persisted for more than two centuries in delicate counterpoise with an equally pervasive obsession with technology and progress—a dichotomy of values which often threatened to, and, indeed, too regularly did, disrupt the pristine sanctity of the American garden. Wilderness, usually best admired from afar, represented above all a challenge to be overcome and bent to man's will. This civilizing process meant that the forests must be cleared, the wild denizens of the woods either tamed or destroyed, and rivers and streams dammed and harnessed to man's purposes. In sum, civilization required that the natural environment be replaced by man's artificial world of neatly trimmed farmlands and self-contained, well-ordered villages and towns to which the farmer might go for living necessities, recreation, and human companionship.[1]

As long as America remained essentially a land of open spaces, family farms, and small towns, deification of unspoiled nature and the virtues allegedly produced by contact with it, and the contradictory desire to alter, if not to destroy it, could coexist without doing violence

1. Excellent analyses of American attitudes toward the pastoral appear in Roderick Nash, *Wilderness and the American Mind;* Henry Nash Smith, *Virgin Land: The American West as Symbol and Myth;* and Richard Hofstadter, *The Age of Reform: From Bryan to F.D.R.*, pp. 23–59.

to the American dream of an ever-increasing good life.[2] The realities of the twentieth century, however, changed all of that. Two great wars, high technology, accelerating industrial production and the accompanying depletion of natural resources, population explosion, and unplanned, chaotic urban sprawl brought the first shocks of remorse and a glimmering suspicion that progress could exact too high a price. Subsequent cold-war confrontations; the ever-present menace of nuclear holocaust; demands by minorities for economic, social, and civil equality; violent racial and class conflicts; and the threat of energy famine added to rising tensions. Caught up in a world they neither understood nor empathized with, many Americans gave vent to an ever-increasing, albeit nostalgic and unrealistic, desire for a return to the "good old days" when people allegedly lived in communal harmony with themselves and with nature.[3]

The Urban Growth and New Community Development Act of 1970, and especially one of its progeny, The Woodlands, is a manifestation of that yearning for harmonious unity of man, community, and nature. In that sense it echoes the nineteenth-century thought of the English urban planner Ebenezer Howard, who wanted the modern city to be a composite of the best qualities of urban and rural life. The revived concept of new towns, an idea traceable to antiquity, embodied in the legislation is also indicative of the growing realization that American cities, and hence the quality of American life, faced bleak prospects unless disparate economic and political interest groups joined together

2. Hofstadter explains this paradox by describing America as "the only country in the world that began with perfection and aspired to progress." Hofstadter, *Age of Reform*, p. 36.

3. Elizabeth Kassler, "New Towns, New Cities," in *The New City: Architecture and Urban Renewal*, p. 9. Kassler contends: "Americans have never had much confidence in city pavements, city crowds, city ways, city slickers. Since industrial cities were necessary to the economy, we built them, but with left hands and half a heart. Jefferson spoke for many of his compatriots when he condemned great cities as 'pestilential to the morals, the health and liberties of men.'" James A. Clapp, *New Towns and Urban Policy: Planning Metropolitan Growth*, p. 1, points out that "historically, Americans appear to have possessed an anti-urban bias, with a tendency to concentrate on the negative qualities of the city." M. Carter McFarland, *Federal Government and Urban Problems: HUD—Successes, Failures, and the Fate of Our Cities*, p. 17, believes that the most important reason for tardy recognition of urban problems "lies deep in American ideology and cultural values. The country has had a nostalgic attachment to rural and small-town images." Gerald Allen, "A Last Word—New Towns: Re-Creation not Transformation," *Architectural Record* 154 (December, 1973): 142, argues that in reality new towns are essentially conservative in that they attempt "to re-create some lost, better forms of urban living and to adapt them to present practicalities and social ideals."

11

to forge a national urban policy aimed at planning and building for a better future.[4]

Urban planning was not, of course, an exclusive phenomenon of the midtwentieth century. The "City Beautiful" movement following the 1893 World's Columbian Exhibition in Chicago in 1893, the "Garden City" concept inspired by Ebenezer Howard, the "Regional City" synthesis formulated and sponsored by the Regional Planning Association of America, and the New Deal's "Green Belt Town" project identified and sought to halt the eroding quality of life perceived in concrete and steel cities essentially devoid of social and environmental amenities. Although none of these attempts at urban planning reform succeeded to the degree hoped for by their advocates, they did nonetheless provide experience and publicize the views of professional architects, engineers, conservationists, ecologists, and social planners, all of whom shared a common belief that cities could be planned so as to provide optimum harmony between man, his community, and nature.[5]

Without question the "Regional City" synthesis articulated by the most distinguished leaders of the Regional Planning Association of America—Lewis Mumford, Benton MacKaye, Clarence Stein, Henry Wright, and Frederick L. Ackerman—made the greatest contribution to the revived new-community concept of the 1960s and 1970s. Most of all, their insistence that private capital could not or would not do the job alone and their demand for greater government involvement, especially in the form of financial assistance, provided a basis for later legislative formulation and implementation.

This central idea stemmed not from a common distaste for capitalistic enterprise but rather from concepts of size and efficient land use which defined the "Regional City" synthesis. First, its advocates, drawing from the "Garden City" idea but going beyond it, emphasized the economic, social, and environmental advantages of large-scale development by "superblocks," neighborhoods, and communities. Second, the "Regional City" concept, borrowing from European and American sources, called for a regional reconstruction designed to harmonize man, community, and nature. This required the establishment of new towns, renewal of existing urban centers, and minimization of man's impact on the countryside. Third, because of the foregoing concepts, and because of the insistence of the Regional Planning Association of

4. Clapp, New Towns and Urban Policy, pp. 15–18, 23–26.

5. Roy Lubove, "The Roots of Urban Planning," in Allen M. Wakstein, ed., The Urbanization of America: An Historical Anthology, pp. 315–29; Joseph L. Arnold, The New Deal in the Suburbs: A History of the Greenbelt Town Program, 1936–1954; Paul K. Conkin, Tomorrow a New World: The New Deal Community Program.

America on the need to exploit and elaborate on new techniques of planning, the availability of long-term, low-cost capital became essential, even paramount, to a program of controlled urban growth.[6]

While urban planners like Lewis Mumford and others continued to press for planned cities during the immediate post–World War II era, their voices essentially went unheard. The first administration of Harry S Truman, beset by a multitude of problems flowing out of demobilization and a cooling of relations with the Soviet Union, failed to cope adequately with either the worsening housing shortage or increasing urban blight. Truman's electoral victory in 1948, however, launched the Fair Deal, one provision of which was to alleviate housing deficiencies and urban decay. The Housing Act of 1949 provided for the construction of 810,000 units of public housing, federal appropriations for slum clearance, and expansion of Federal Housing Administration (FHA) mortgage loans and mortgage insurance. The act, labeled by some observers as Truman's finest legislative achievement and by others as "neither generous nor comprehensive, only painfully inadequate," failed to achieve its major goal of a "decent home in a suitable environment for every American family."[7]

The fiscally cautious administration of President Dwight D. Eisenhower likewise failed to confront the deepening sickness of urban slums and the social alienation of people without homes or hope. Indeed, Eisenhower's insistence on a massive federal-state highway construction program unwittingly greatly contributed to urban blight and the flight to suburbia. Although embraced by many city planners as the ultimate solution to inner-city revitalization, the Federal Aid Highway Act of 1956 also elicited despair and gloomy predictions from other experts like Lewis Mumford, who sadly commented, "The most charitable thing to assume about this [legislation] is that they hadn't the faintest notion of what they were doing." Mumford also accurately predicted that the inherent error of the program would eventually be acknowledged, but, he added, "too late to correct all the damage to our cities and our countryside."[8] Mumford proved to be all too prescient.

6. Roy Lubove, "The Roots of Urban Planning," pp. 326–29.
7. Robert Griffith, "Truman and the Historians: The Reconstruction of Postwar American History," *Wisconsin Magazine of History* 59 (Autumn, 1975): 37–38. Griffith points out that of the authorized 810,000 units of public housing only 60,000 were built during Truman's administration. Fifteen years later the total had risen to just 365,000. Griffith ascribes Truman's failure to "bureaucratic timidity, a lack of presidential leadership, the Korean War, and the vigorous opposition of real estate interests."
8. Quoted in Richard O. Davies, *The Age of Asphalt: The Automobile, the Freeway, and the Condition of Metropolitan America,* p. 24.

The resultant razing of inner-city neighborhoods, usually occupied by poverty-level ethnic minorities; the dissecting of lower- and middle-class residential areas; and the paving over of parks and open spaces to accommodate gigantic highway cloverleafs, expressways, parking areas, and feeder streets caused even greater urban blight. The creation of freeway networks also increased the flight to suburbia, where real estate developers took advantage of the opportunity provided by improved highway systems into the hinterlands to build even more undistinguished, standardized homes. Urban planner and transportation expert Wilfred Owen succinctly expressed the dilemma: "Where all-out efforts have been made to accommodate the car, the streets are still congested, commuting is increasingly difficult, urban aesthetics have suffered, and the quality of life has been eroded. In an automotive age, cities have become the negation of communities—a setting for machines instead of people. . . . The automobile is an irresistible force that may become an immovable object, and in the process destroy the city."[9] John W. Lawrence, dean of Tulane University's School of Architecture, struck an equally somber note when he admonished, "The entrances to our city are a disgrace—something to despoil the spirit and cause one to die a little every time they are traversed. . . . That men could wreak such vulgarity upon their neighbors with the full support of law is both shocking and prophetic of decline."[10]

The pendulum which thus far in the post–World War II period had swung consistently toward either inadequate or destructive programs affecting American cities slowly reversed itself with the advent of President John F. Kennedy's New Frontier and President Lyndon B. Johnson's Great Society. Kennedy has been described as the first American president who did not reflect the rural bias of the American people. Although he failed in his 1962 bid to establish a cabinet-level urban department, according to one political scientist, "Kennedy will be remembered for many things but in the long run, it may well be that he will be best remembered as the first President to understand the importance of the metropolitan revolution in the United States and as the first to try to do something about it."[11]

Johnson's program, with its emphasis on improvement in the quality of life of all Americans, attempted to squarely address the pressing problems stemming from urban decay, first through the Housing and

9. Ibid.
10. Quoted in Milton D. Speizman, ed., *Urban America in the Twentieth Century*, p. 220.

11. McFarland, *Federal Government and Urban Problems*, p. 17.

Urban Development Act of 1965 and then through creation of a cabinet-level Department of Housing and Urban Development (HUD).[12] The president's message to Congress urging the creation of an agency to administer the various federal urban programs went beyond the issue at hand and prophetically iterated the guiding philosophy behind the Urban Growth and New Community Acts of 1968 and 1970. Johnson stated:

> Let us be clear about the core of this problem. The problem is people and the quality of lives they lead. We want to build not just housing units, but neighborhoods; not just to construct schools, but to educate children; not just to raise income, but to create beauty and end the poisoning of our environment. The city should be a place where every man feels safe on his streets and in the house of his friends. It should be a place where each individual's dignity and self-respect is strengthened by the respect and affection of his neighbors. It should be a place where each of us can find the satisfaction and warmth which comes only from being a member of the community of men. This is what man sought at the dawn of civilization. It is what we seek today.[13]

Johnson's words and his vision of better American cities, plus the frightening realities of riots in Watts (1965), Chicago (1966), and Tampa, Cincinnati, Atlanta, and New Brunswick (1967), prompted the introduction in Congress of several bills aimed at urban reform. In congressional hearings conducted on proposed legislation which in final form became the Housing and Urban Development Act of 1968, witness after witness affirmed support for a comprehensive program of housing and urban reform and especially for a program of federal financial incentives to private developers of new communities. James Rouse, president of Urban America, Inc., and of the Rouse Company, provided the legislators with an informative account of his company's huge capital investment, all from private sources, in the development of Columbia, Maryland, a 14,000-acre, "color-blind," environmentally aesthetic new community midway between Baltimore and Washington, D.C. Rouse, citing the National Advisory Committee on Civil Disorders' "chilling diagnosis of the current conditions of the cities," also delivered a plea for enactment of experimental and innovative federal programs, such as financial assistance to new-town developers who in turn

12. Arthur S. Link and William B. Catton, *American Epoch: A History of the United States since the 1890's*, III, 889.
13. Lyndon B. Johnson, *Message on Cities—Message from the President of the United States*, H. Doc. 99; reprinted in Speizman, ed., *Urban America*, pp. 225, 228.

would be required to provide low- and moderate-income housing. Such action, Rouse hoped, would aid in the forging of a comprehensive national strategy to counteract the forces of division and disorder which plagued the nation in the 1960s.[14]

Despite the support given by Rouse and others to large-scale, federally aided new communities, the House Subcommittee on Housing reported a bill which omitted provisions for new towns. In the Senate, where a deeper sense of urgency and willingness to experiment punctuated debate, Charles Percy of Illinois pointed to the perennial split between those he characterized as "housing people" and "people people" which customarily frustrated every attempt to adopt a comprehensive housing program. "Any effort," Percy warned, "to achieve both human and physical renewal for low-income families and neighborhoods . . . must find a way to bridge this gap. . . . We must . . . consider the needs of the 'whole man' and provide programs which . . . provide homes, not just housing." Wisconsin's Senator William Proxmire joined Percy in his support of new-community legislation and reminded his colleagues that the proposed federal guarantees and supplemental grants totaling a maximum of $500 million were conditional upon a developer providing a substantial number of homes for low- and moderate-income families. "If," Proxmire cautioned, "we are to assist in the planning and establishment of new communities and new towns we must strive to insure that the plan provides for low and moderate income housing as well as upper income housing."[15] Sen. John Tower of Texas, who during the debate alternated between professions of deep concern for low-income families and a more typical fiscal conservatism, capped his enigmatic stand by offering an amendment designed to delete Title IV (the New Community Act) from the bill. Tower argued:

> I cannot concur with a program of Government guarantees for the development of entirely new communities. . . . This is no time for us to guarantee $500,000,000 to speculative schemes involving the new communities. . . . There have been a number of these that have sprung up all over the country, and I do not know of any that have been a great financial success. At a time when we should be addressing ourselves to the problems of existing urban areas, why should we go chasing off after a scheme to build new communities?[16]

14. U.S. Congress, House, *Housing and Urban Development Legislation and Urban Insurance; Hearings before a Subcommittee on Housing of the Committee on Banking and Currency*, 90th Cong., 2nd sess. (1968), pp. 982, 988–89.

15. *Congressional Record*, 90th Cong., 2nd sess. (1968), 15266–70.

16. Ibid., 15118, 15122. Tower had previously joined two of his colleagues in a

The failure of Tower's amendment prompted Sen. Peter H. Dominick of Colorado to introduce an amendment reducing the total amount of government guarantees to developers of new towns from $500 million to $250 million. Dominick supported his proposed reduction by quoting statistics gleaned from a 1966 magazine article on the financial woes and failures of four privately developed new towns – Reston, Virginia; El Dorado Hills, California; Clear Lake City, Texas; and, Columbia, Maryland. In each instance except Columbia, which had not yet broken ground, home sales had fallen dismally short of projections despite large capital investments in land, amenities, public utilities, access streets, and construction. While the object lesson of the article in fact supported the oft-repeated admonition of James Rouse and others that financing of new communities required a relatively long period of deferred principal repayment money for the developers, the senators opted for frugality and approved the reduction before giving overwhelming approval to the measure.[17]

In the House, after a substitution of its own proposal for the approved Senate bill, the debate also focused on civil disorders and the urgency of remedial action. Congressman Wright Patman of Texas observed that "over the past few years this country has become painfully aware of the problems besieging our cities. We have lived through a period of needless and destructive violence." But, he warned, "it is important we recognize that these problems are not new. They were not the creation of four summers. They are the inheritance of 100 years of growth and neglect."[18] Patman's support of reform legislation reflected both his concern for the disadvantaged in American society and the influence of his colleague from Ohio, Thomas L. Ashley.

Ashley's thorough disenchantment with traditional, unplanned urban development dated back a decade. He also recognized the futility of advocating any program which seemed to threaten American concepts of private property. Ashley later recalled: "I wanted to try to take on the traditional development process. It was very clear to me that this would be impossible for me to do alone or even in concert with like-minded members of Congress because of the entrenched interests which were far too strong . . . the National Association of Home Build-

report stating their objections to the Senate Committee on Housing and Urban Affairs bill. "We cannot agree," the senators wrote, "with those who maintain that America's cities are so sick that their only chance for improvement rests in total reliance on the Federal Government." See *Housing and Urban Development Act of 1968*, S. Rep. 1123, 90th Cong., 2nd sess., p. 177.

17. *Congressional Record*, 90th Cong., 2nd sess. (1968), 15266–70.
18. Ibid., 20061, 20562, 20597.

ers and the National Association of Real Estate Boards." To succeed against such opposition, and to avoid violating the sanctity of private property, Ashley concluded that "we would have to find a different mechanism, a different kind of approach, and . . . new communities . . . seemed to lend themselves to this."[19]

In pursuit of that strategy Ashley seconded Patman's expression of the urgency of reform and added, "My principal disappointment in the bill . . . is that it does not provide for . . . aid to developers of new communities. . . . Certainly we must direct a massive effort to the rehabilitation of existing urban centers, but if we are to avoid compounding these very problems in our suburbs and rural communities, we must encourage the kind of preventive planning and action adopted in the [Senate's] housing bill."[20] Ashley and like-minded members of the House undoubtedly took solace, however, in the thought, expressed by New York's William F. Ryan, that the new-community program might be salvaged in conference committee. The hope did not prove illusory. The Senate refused to accept the House amendment, and the subsequent conference committee report included the previously stricken Title IV, which provided federal aid to developers of new towns. Despite vocal opposition from some members, the House approved the measure by a wide margin on July 26, 1968, one day after Senate approval.[21]

The New Community Act of 1968 failed to fulfill the expectations of its supporters during its short life for two reasons. First, the financial incentives offered by the act did not prove attractive enough to elicit applications for aid by a significant number of developers. Second, the incoming administration of Richard M. Nixon, including the new secretary of housing and urban development, George Romney, preferred different, though not clearly specified, approaches to urban reform. The vagueness of the administration's urban program plus the recognized failure of the 1968 act to stimulate new-community development produced yet another spate of legislative proposals and inspired two years of congressional hearings preparatory to passage of the Urban Growth and New Community Development Act of 1970.

Despite President Nixon's call in his 1970 State of the Union message for more attractive federal financial incentives to new-community developers, when legislation providing additional inducements reached the House floor in September, 1970, administration forces waged a determined battle for deletion.[22] Congressman Ashley, already acclaimed

19. Quoted in Carlos C. Campbell, *New Towns: Another Way to Live,* p. 196.
20. *Congressional Record,* 90th Cong., 2nd sess. (1968), 20082.
21. Ibid., 20087, 23636–82, 23686, 23688, 23691.
22. *State of the Union Message, President Richard M. Nixon,* January 20, 1970, H.

as the father of the new-community provisions (Title I) of the proposed House bill, recalled during the protracted debate that he had met with Secretary Romney several times before the final writing of the measure in an attempt to reconcile known administration objections. He had subsequently acquiesced to two changes: his proposed Community Development Corporation would be inside rather than outside HUD, and federal incentives would take the form of guarantees of bonds and other obligations rather than direct loans to new-community developers.[23] Nonetheless, administration opposition persisted, ostensibly because it sought to "consolidate, simplify and rationalize" federal housing programs while the Ashley bill contained provisions considered to be "novel, complex and controversial."[24] Apprised of these misgivings in the executive branch, Congressman Robert G. Stephens, Jr., of Georgia offered a substitute for the Ashley bill which eliminated the urban-growth council opposed by the administration and directed the president to utilize his domestic council instead. It also reduced the cost of the total program from approximately $7 billion to $2.8 billion. Not satisfied with this attempt at compromise, and unquestionably speaking for the administration, Congressman Garry Brown, a member of the Housing Subcommittee, where he had voted for the Ashley bill, offered a substitute amendment which Pennsylvania's William A. Barrett correctly observed "completely nullified" the new-community program. Brown's amendment failed, but on the following day the representatives approved an amendment by Lawrence G. Williams of Pennsylvania to strike all of Title I. Thus shorn of a major provision, the bill won approval.[25]

In the Senate the emasculated Ashley bill won quick approval after the addition of an insignificant amendment, but House refusal to accept the amendment necessitated appointment of a conference committee. To the chagrin of some House members and the delight of others,

---

Doc. 91–226, 91st Cong., 2nd sess., p. 8. President Nixon stated in part: "Between now and the year 2,000 over one-hundred-million children will be born in the United States. Where they grow up—and how—will, more than any one thing, measure the quality of American life in these years ahead. This should be a warning to us. . . . The violent and decayed central cities of our great metropolitan complexes are the most conspicuous area of failure in American life. I propose that before these problems become insoluble, the nation develop a national growth policy. . . . In particular the Federal government must be in a position to assist in the building of new cities and the rebuilding of old ones."

23. *Congressional Record*, 91st Cong., 2nd sess. (1970), 39461–62.

24. George Romney to Garry Brown, December 1, 1970, printed in ibid., 39465.

25. *Congressional Record*, 91st Cong., 2nd sess. (1970), 39479–99, 39505, 39828, 39831.

19

the committee's report included Title VII, better known as the New Community Act of 1970. Amid charges of surrender and even betrayal the House approved the conference report on December 19, one day after Senate affirmation.[26]

In its final form the New Community Act offered federal financial assistance to private developers of new towns in the form of guarantees of bonds, debentures, notes, and other obligations issued by developers to finance land purchases and land development. A single project could not receive guarantees in excess of $50 million, and the aggregate amount guaranteed under the program could not exceed $500 million. To further aid developers, the act authorized the Community Development Corporation, created within HUD, to administer the new-communities program and to make fifteen-year interest-free loans up to a maximum of $20 million to enable developers to pay interest charges on indebtedness resulting from land purchases and land development. The total amount of such loans could not exceed $240 million. In addition, the act authorized the Community Development Corporation to provide supplemental and public service grants to local public bodies assisting in the development of the communities. Finally, the secretary could provide financial aid for planning costs in excess of those needed to establish the market, financial, and engineering feasibility of a project.[27]

To be eligible for these various forms of financial aid, a proposed new community had to meet the following criteria:

(1) [It] will provide an alternative to disorderly urban growth, helping preserve or enhance desirable aspects of the natural and urban environment or so improving general and economic conditions in established communities as to help reverse migration from existing cities or rural areas;
(2) will be economically feasible in terms of economic base or potential for economic growth;
(3) will contribute to the welfare of the entire area which will be substantially affected by the program and of which the land to be developed is a part;
(4) is consistent with comprehensive planning, physical and social, determined by the Secretary to provide an adequate basis of evaluating the new community development program in relation to other plans (including State, local, and private plans) and activities involving area pop-

26. Ibid., 40458–59, 40916, 41339, 42299–42314, 42316, 42438, 42442, 42629–31, 42635, 42637.

27. *U.S. Statutes at Large,* 84: 1791–1805.

ulation, housing and development trends, and transportation, water, sewerage, open space, recreation, and other relevant facilities;

(5) has received all governmental reviews and approvals required by State or local law, or by the Secretary;

(6) will contribute to good living conditions in the community, and that such community will be characterized by well balanced and diversified land use patterns and will include or be served by adequate public, community, and commercial facilities (including facilities needed for education, health and social services, recreation, and transportation) deemed satisfactory by the Secretary;

(7) makes substantial provision for housing within the means of persons of low and moderate income and that such housing will constitute an appropriate proportion of the community's housing supply; and

(8) will make significant use of advances in design and technology with respect to land utilization, materials and methods of construction, and the provision of community facilities and services.[28]

In retrospect the New Community Act of 1970 from its inception faced difficult odds. Both it and its predecessor, the New Community Act of 1968, won congressional approval not by a clear and enthusiastic mandate but because of the determination and parliamentary skills of a hard-core minority, especially in the lower house, who outmaneuvered less skillful and often ambivalent opponents. Like any other sickly infant, if it was to flourish and grow, the New Community Act required vigilant and constant nurture. Thrust into the grudging care of an uncommitted administration and an agency totally inexperienced in the new responsibilities with which it was charged, rife with internal power struggles, and extraordinarily prone to excessive leadership and staff turnovers, the chances of the New Community Act to survive, let alone succeed, looked slim indeed.

28. Ibid., 1796.

3. Genesis of a New Town

LAND ACQUISITION AND ECOLOGICAL AND ECONOMIC PLANNING, 1964–1971

The chaotic and distressing national urban scene of the early 1960s in no small way contributed to congressional determination to put the money and the power of the federal government to work building better American cities. The decade 1960 to 1970 also witnessed a continuation of the unparalleled economic boom of the 1950s. The Houston area not only shared in that prosperity but surpassed it as the decade progressed. Real estate speculation, always a favorite enterprise of Houston's business community, promised untold rewards to those with the capital and the foresight to invest in the right areas. By a happy turn of fortune, and some shrewdness on his part, George Mitchell's decision to invest in undeveloped land coincided with greater government involvement in urban improvement and near-runaway population and economic growth in the Houston metropolitan area.

Mitchell's thinking as he led his company into increased land investments beginning in 1964 apparently had not progressed beyond that of the typical speculator who thought in terms of small-scale development and quick profit. By that time a number of factors had convinced him that the area northwest of Houston offered the greatest opportunity for a profitable return on investment: Houston's previous and existing growth pattern placed it in the path of greatest future expansion; major highway conduits served the area—Farm to Market Road (FM) 1960 from east to west and a major north-south artery, Interstate 45, leading to Dallas; and, just east of the junction of these two major thoroughfares the new Houston Intercontinental Airport was scheduled for completion in 1968.

Before 1960 the southeast and southwest sectors dominated Houston's industrial, residential, and population growth. The northwest area, including northern Harris and southern Montgomery counties, remained essentially rural because of distance from Houston and difficulty of access. Champions, the first major residential project in the region, started slowly because of the time-consuming motor trip through a jumble of narrow, winding streets lined with shacks and auto junkyards. Completion of I-45 early in the decade quickened the pace of Champions' development and contributed to a gradual shift of major population growth away from the southeast-southwest and into the northwest quadrant. The subsequent development of several residential subdivisions near the periphery of downtown Houston — Shepherd Park Plaza, Chateau Forest, Willow Run, North Plaza, and Greenridge — plus additional suburbs farther north, including Ponderosa Forest, Huntwick, Memorial Hills, Inverness, Enchanted Oaks, North Hampton, Memorial Northwest, Timber Ridge, and River Plantation — contributed to a growth which swelled total population in the northwest quadrant to 423,000 by 1970.[1]

A concurrent expansion in the number of retail outlets, light industries, service-related enterprises, and hotel-motels further transformed the northwest region, particularly during the last three years of the decade. Completion of two large shopping malls, Northline in 1962 and Northwest in 1968, plus six smaller centers increased retail outlets from 141 to 363 and added to the bustling commercial activity in the region, as did a rise in hotel-motel space from 282 rooms in 1962 to 1,455 in 1970.[2]

The city of Conroe and southern Montgomery County also benefited from a land boom comparable to the rush generated by the Conroe oil strike of the 1930s. By spring, 1964, nearly three thousand homesites were strung out along ten miles of freeway from the southern boundary of the county to Conroe plus about seventy-five subdivisions scattered throughout the vicinity competed for prospective buyers. The

1. *Houston Chronicle,* February 6, 1973; "Ready to Roll," *Houston* 31 (September, 1960): 56; Gladstone Associates, Metropolitan Economic Background, Mitchell-Houston New Community, p. 6; Gladstone Associates, Market Opportunities, Mitchell-Houston New Community, p. 23.

2. Gladstone Associates, Market Opportunities, pp. 50–51, 65, 69. Industrial-park acreage in the region increased by 100 percent from 1967 to 1969. Most of the increase — 2,100 of 2,300 acres — was in the Intercontinental Airport Industrial Park.

The Woodlands site in relation to the Houston metropolitan area and major highway-airport facilities.

plentiful supply of desirable wooded tracts and the recreation potential of Lake Conroe, a 21,000-acre lake created by a dam on the San Jacinto River begun in the summer of 1964, continued to attract newcomers throughout the 1960s and accounted for most of Montgomery County's 77 percent population increase during the decade.[3]

The positive qualities of the northwest area mentioned above caused

3. Charles A. Warner, *Texas Oil and Gas since 1543*, pp. 212, 369; *Houston Post*, May 1, 1964; Gladstone Associates, Metropolitan Economic Background, pp. 140, 142–43.

Mitchell to obtain options to purchase two thousand acres near the intersection of FM 1960 and I-45. The passage of time and further examination, however, revealed major negative factors. Champions, a high-income, country-club-oriented real estate project, already claimed much of the remaining desirable land. Furthermore, commercial development along FM 1960 and I-45 increasingly evidenced a high degree of blight marked by a hodgepodge of fast-food chains and retail outlets. Those faults, plus Mitchell's slowly maturing plans for a large-scale development, led him to allow his purchase options to lapse in favor of a move farther north. "We gave up," Mitchell later recalled, "because it was too fragmented, too difficult to put together. I figured if we didn't have five to seven thousand acres, we couldn't do even the beginning of what we had talked about doing."[4]

Mitchell then turned his attention to a largely undeveloped, wooded area in southern Montgomery County about ten miles north of the intersection of FM 1960 and I-45. In May, 1964, his firm had purchased the Grogan-Cochran Lumber Company and its 50,000 acres of timberlands in Montgomery, Liberty, Waller, and Grimes counties for $6,250,000, or an average price of $125 an acre. At that time development of the purchase presented several alternatives: preparation of lake, ranch, and farm sites; small residential or recreational subdivisions; or future oil-and-gas explorations. Later, when the full dimensions of a new-town project had taken shape, 2,800 acres of the Grogan-Cochran land served as the nucleus.[5]

In April, 1966, Mitchell's agents approached the Roman Catholic Diocese of Galveston-Houston, owner of the Blanche Foley tract, comprising 1,070 acres in southern Montgomery County. Serious negotiations for a purchase commenced in December, 1967, and continued until March 8, 1970, after Mitchell's decision to apply for federal aid under the 1968 new-town legislation. The sale agreement provided for a primarily cash transaction but included an important proviso: at some future date the diocese could select 70 acres within the intended project for the construction of religious or educational facilities.[6]

The purchase of the Sutton-Mann tract of four thousand acres re-

4. Interview with George P. Mitchell, October 16, 1979.

5. "The Woodlands Chronicle" (undated manuscript in Woodlands Development Corporation Papers, The Woodlands, Tex.), pp. 1–3, hereafter cited as WDC Papers; interview with Charles Lively, August 6, 1980; interview with Paul W. Wommack, November 1, 1982; *Houston Post,* May 12, 1964. The *Post* reported that the average price per acre was "about $130."

6. Interview with Paul W. Wommack, November 1, 1982; "The Woodlands Chronicle," p. 3.

quired equally time-consuming and complex negotiations. Robert Mann, an East Texas banker, drove a hard bargain, since parts of the tract fronted I-45 and therefore controlled access to the project. Negotiations continued for more than three years before being completed in September, 1972. Those portions of the purchase which fronted on I-45 sold for fifty cents a square foot, the most costly of the lands eventually included in the project. Banker Mann also insisted on a proviso in the sales contract that he would be given the right of first refusal should facilities for a second bank become necessary in the project during the ensuing ten years.[7]

Another significant acquisition involved not a conventional purchase contract but a trade of lands. The Champion Paper Corporation owned forty-three hundred acres of land in the project area. Champion indicated a desire to dispose of its holdings if an exchange of suitable timberlands owned elsewhere by the Mitchell interests could be arranged. Negotiations began in February, 1968, and were completed in October, 1970. During the lengthy discussions Champion's representatives contended that a trade could not be made on a one-for-one basis because of the greater value of the company's lands within the project's confines. Mitchell's agents reluctantly conceded the point, and the final agreement exchanged Champion's forty-three hundred acres inside the project for twelve thousand acres of Mitchell timberlands held elsewhere.[8]

The Grogan-Cochran, Galveston-Houston Diocese, Sutton-Mann, and Champion Paper Company tracts represented the largest transactions, but they certainly did not constitute the entire land-acquisition process. On the contrary, most of the land purchases involved tracts of less than twenty-five acres, requiring an estimated five hundred separate transactions. This obviously entailed a tremendous amount of time spent not only on administrative and legal matters but also on often delicate negotiations which demanded large amounts of tact and diplomacy. Mitchell, while closely involved in all these matters, was assisted by Charles Lively, his acquisitions agent; David Bumgardner, a company attorney; and Paul Wommack, Mitchell's chief legal adviser.

Mitchell's staff found most of the landowners willing to sell at a fair price. If negotiations faltered over the sales price, Mitchell instructed his agents to meet the owner's demands unless they were grossly exorbitant. He also instructed his agents to inform a prospective seller from

7. "The Woodlands Chronicle," pp. 3–4; interview with Paul W. Wommack, November 1, 1982.

8. Interview with Paul W. Wommack, November 1, 1982; interview with Charles Lively, August 5, 1980.

the outset of negotiations that they represented the Mitchell interests. This openness contributed considerably to the success of most
negotiations.[9]

Land costs varied, of course, depending on the size of the purchase
and its strategic location within the project. The early Grogan-Cochran
purchase, it will be recalled, averaged $125 an acre. Parts of the Sutton-
Mann tract, with its control of access to I-45, sold for $.50 a square
foot, or nearly $22,000 an acre. For the project as a whole land-purchase
costs averaged $1,688 an acre.[10]

Within the approximately 20,000 acres then embraced by the project, twelve "out parcels," or "holes," totaling 692 acres remained whose
owners refused to sell.[11] A few of them demanded exorbitant prices.
Most refused to sell at any price because of long-term family ownership or because the land represented a home, a hunting lodge, or a
weekend retreat in a sylvan setting removed from the pressures of urban life — ironically evidencing some of the same spirit that motivated
George Mitchell to initiate his project.[12]

Early in 1966, while he was consolidating his landholdings in
southern Montgomery County, Mitchell began discussing a design for
a possible new community with Karl Kamrath, a Houston architect,
who had designed Mitchell's home and many other Houston projects.
Discussion quickly moved beyond speculation, and in March, 1966,
Kamrath's firm, MacKie, Kamrath, and Pickford Planning Development
Associates, submitted a completed plan to Mitchell. Kamrath's proposal
contemplated a community embracing twenty thousand acres with a
population of fifty thousand. In no way innovative, the town plan included the traditional central shopping mall surrounded by single-family
residential areas with multiple-family units and light industry on the
peripheries.[13]

At this point Mitchell knew little about the large-scale, planned

9. Interview with Charles Lively, August 6, 1980.
10. "Nobody's Laughing Now," Forbes 127 (March 2, 1978): 84. The article also points
out that the value of the land appreciated rapidly: "Mitchell bought the land at an average of $1,688 an acre, then spent $25,000 an acre more to develop it. Today, the average
Woodlands acre sells for $62,000 with the choicest going for up to $152,000. The Woodlands is only 22% developed today. When fully developed, even if the land never appreciated further, it could go on the market at $1 billion."
11. Indenture of Mortgage and Deed of Trust, The Woodlands Development Corporation to the Chase Manhattan Bank, Trustee, August 23, 1972, p. 19.
12. However, each owner of an out parcel signed a "right of first refusal" agreement. Should the owner decide to sell at a future date, the owner must give Mitchell
the first opportunity to buy the land. "The Woodlands Chronicle," p. 5.
13. Ibid., p. 2.

communities already begun by Robert Simon at Reston, Virginia, and on the drawing board at Columbia, Maryland, under the direction of James Rouse. His growing interest in the potential of new-town development, however, caused him to probe further. Two factors prompted his decision to explore more fully: he knew that at least limited federal financial aid could be obtained under Title X of the 1965 housing act, and the increasingly volatile condition of the oil-and-gas industry, at least for independents, convinced him of the need to find new avenues of investment for Mitchell Energy and Development Corporation.[14] He therefore continued to consolidate his landholdings and in December, 1968, four months after the Urban Growth and New Community Act became law, began discussions with another Houston architect, Cerf Ross, about designing a new town. Ross completed a plan as 1969 drew to a close. His projected new town of nearly fifteen thousand acres included a lake, a golf course, an industrial park, and a university campus. Ross's plan departed in a major way from the earlier Kamrath design through inclusion of four distinct residential communities around a central business complex.[15]

Although early in the gestation period Mitchell had thought in terms of seeking private financial backing for his new town, in February, 1970, he submitted a proposal incorporating the Ross plan to HUD for aid under the Urban Growth and New Community Act of 1968.[16] Neither Mitchell nor other prospective new-town developers knew of HUD's ultraconservative approach to approvals under the law (only two, Jonathan, Minnesota, and St. Charles, Maryland, received authorization during the life of the 1968 law). By the same token Mitchell did not know that strengthening legislation—the Urban Growth and New Community Development Act of 1970—was then running the congressional gauntlet. In early June, 1970, he learned from contacts in HUD that the Ross proposal lacked sufficient professional planning, but on June 17, William Nicoson, director of HUD's Office of New Community Development, approved the preapplication proposal and invited Mitchell to submit a formal application.[17]

14. Interview with George P. Mitchell, October 16, 1979.
15. "The Woodlands Chronicle," p. 13.
16. Interview with George P. Mitchell, October 16, 1979. By this time Mitchell had spent $100,000 on planning. "The Woodlands Chronicle," p. 13.
17. "The Woodlands Chronicle," p. 14. An official from HUD informed J. A. McAlister that The Woodlands project was in every way outstanding with one exception—"the conceptualization. . . ." He also stated that he would "regret to see the application rejected because of weakness in this one area." J. A. McAlister to George P. Mitchell, June 5, 1970, in the McAlister Company, Reading File on New Town Project, Houston, Tex.

Thus encouraged, and informed of shortcomings in the Ross proposal, Mitchell began assembling a consulting team capable of providing the professional expertise required to comply with the multifaceted goals of new-community legislation and HUD's regulations.

As he cast his net for premier architectural, marketing, engineering, and environmental planners, Mitchell for a time considered several Houston firms but eventually rejected most on the basis of limited experience for a project on the scale he now intended. One such firm, Caudill, Rowlett, Scott, included in its ranks a young urban-development specialist, Robert J. Hartsfield, who enjoyed the distinction of having studied under Ian McHarg, a renowned ecologist and urban planner at the University of Pennsylvania. Hartsfield's credentials plus his demonstrated professionalism persuaded Mitchell to woo him away from Caudill, Rowlett, Scott and onto his staff as director of planning and design. Hartsfield proved a happy choice; among other contributions he suggested that Mitchell read McHarg's *Design with Nature,* an experience which Mitchell later said opened entirely new vistas to him and led to the selection of McHarg as environmental consultant.[18]

In October, 1970, after several weeks of screening potential consulting firms, Mitchell, Hartsfield, and James McAlister, Mitchell's director of real estate, made their final selections: Gladstone Associates, of Washington, D.C. (economics and marketing); William L. Pereira Associates, of Los Angeles (master planning and design); Richard P. Browne Associates, of Columbia, Maryland (development, engineering, and HUD liaison); and, Wallace, McHarg, Roberts and Todd, of Philadelphia (environmental planning). Each of the firms chosen, and particularly their major partners, possessed national and even international reputations in their specialties. William L. Pereira counted among his achievements the planning and design of new towns at Irvine, California; at Dearborn, Michigan; and on the Ivory Coast of Africa. Richard P. Browne, in addition to political experience as mayor of Wayne, New Jersey, had served as engineering consultant at Columbia, Maryland. Ian McHarg's reputation as an ecologist, landscape architect, and urban planner rested on numerous articles, his position as chairman of the University of Pennsylvania's Department of Landscape Architecture and Regional Planning, and his *Design with Nature.* Robert L. Gladstone had participated in planning for Columbia, Maryland, and several other new towns.[19]

18. "The Woodlands Chronicle," p. 14; interview with George P. Mitchell, October 16, 1979.

19. "The Woodlands Chronicle," p. 15; *Woodlands Newsletter,* March–April, 1973, p. 5; May–June, 1973, p. 3.

William L. Pereira, planning consultant, master plan and design.

On October 23, 1970, at the first meeting of the consultants and Mitchell's staff, which had been joined by David Hendricks, previously a management consultant for the Rouse Company at Columbia, almost all revealed an inclination to be involved in more aspects of the planning process than Mitchell intended. Eventually, as Mitchell initially desired, the consultants agreed that each should submit an independent proposal to Mitchell detailing the scope of his group's involvement and the fee expected.[20]

More than three months elapsed before all the consultants, including McHarg's group, had submitted proposals and agreed to contracts. McHarg joined Mitchell's planning team with a well-established reputation for "flamboyant rhetoric" and independence and as an ecolo-

20. "The Woodlands Chronicle," pp. 15, 17.

Richard P. Browne, planning consultant, development and engineering.

gist–urban planner who "puts nature before profit."[21] A native of Scotland, McHarg spent his childhood and adolescence in unspoiled countryside ten miles from Glasgow, an industrial city which he later described as "one of the most implacable testaments of the city of toil in all of Christendom, a memorial to an inordinate capacity to create ugliness, a sandstone excretion cemented with smoke and grime."[22] At age sixteen McHarg, whose early affinity with nature was enhanced by youthful treks through the Black Woods, a mile from his home, decided to become a landscape architect. World War II and service as an officer in a parachute brigade intervened, but with the war's end

21. Dennis Farley, "Land Politics: Ian McHarg," *Atlantic Monthly* 233 (January, 1974): 12.
22. Ian McHarg, *Design with Nature*, pp. 1–5.

Ian McHarg, planning consultant, environmental planning.

he enrolled in Harvard University, where he earned bachelor's and master's degrees in landscape architecture and a master's degree in city planning.

Upon returning to Scotland, where he hoped to "practice [my] faith upon that environment of drudgery that is the Clydeside," McHarg discovered that Glasgow's sprawl had obliterated the Black Woods and to his further dismay learned that he had contracted pulmonary tuberculosis. After six dreary months in a "colony for consumptives" outside Edinburgh, McHarg gained admission to a sanatorium in the Swiss Alps, a six-month experience which affirmed his belief that "sun and sea, orchards in bloom, mountains and snow, fields of flowers, speak to the spirit as well as the flesh."[23]

23. Ibid.

After joining the faculty of the University of Pennsylvania's Department of Landscape Architecture and Regional Planning, McHarg rose rapidly in the ranks of his profession and in 1969 published his most important work, *Design with Nature,* in which he articulated and demonstrated the concept of "ecological determinism," the idea that the ecosystem of any area offers both opportunities and constraints for various kinds of land use. In McHarg's words, "Let us abandon the self-mutilation which has been our way and give expression to the potential harmony of man-nature. The world is abundant; we require only a deference born of understanding to fulfill man's promise. Man is that uniquely conscious creature who can perceive and express. He must become the steward of the biosphere. To do this he must design with nature."[24]

McHarg's description of merchants as "obsequious and insidious" men whose "ethos . . . sustains the slumlord and the land rapist, the polluters of rivers, and the atmosphere" encouraged portrayals of him as an uncompromising idealogue. His advice to a concerned matron who asked him what she could do about pollution — that she should find the president of United States Steel, pounce on him, and "bite him on the jugular"— added to this perception.[25] His image as a rigid anti-business iconoclast, plus his statement at the first consultants' meeting that a large percentage of The Woodlands should not be developed, caused some apprehension in the Mitchell group as they awaited his preliminary ecological report. They might have breathed more easily if they had better understood, rhetoric to the contrary, that McHarg's ecological determinism was not a mechanical, dictatorial system which excluded compromise but provided viable alternatives for land use based on a cost-benefit scale. His preliminary report, delivered to the Mitchell group on March 14, 1971, in a private session during a seminar at Columbia, Maryland, did much to quiet their fears. Upon completion of all necessary ecological studies, McHarg informed them, his report would delineate which lands should be retained as open space and which areas could be developed and to what degree. He also expressed his belief that the site offered unique opportunities for innovative storm-drainage, sewer, and transportation systems.[26]

From the time he first seriously contemplated building a new town,

24. Ibid., p. 5; Jonathan Barnett, "How Are 'Planned Communities' Planned? Designing New Communities," *Architectural Record* 154 (December, 1973): 123, observes that McHarg's theories "seem so eminently sensible that it is hard to understand why they have not been accepted practice for many years."

25. McHarg, *Design with Nature,* p. 25; Farley, "Land Politics: Ian McHarg," p. 12.

26. "The Woodlands Chronicle," pp. 22–23.

33

Mitchell believed that the forest would be its primary asset and therefore must be retained to the highest degree compatible with making a profit. All the consultants shared that opinion, and, not surprisingly, their respective reports emphasized the forest both as an amenity and as a marketing feature.

McHarg's ecological planning study, submitted to Mitchell on July 5, 1971, and later to HUD as a supporting document for the new-community proposal, as well as subsequent, more elaborate studies that he conducted on development phases, also stressed the forest. Because the site posed special, even unique, problems because of its flatness, poorly drained soils, and the presence of streams subject to very low base and very high peak flows, he equally emphasized maintenance of the hydrologic cycle as a key determinant for development.[27] To arrive at his ultimate recommendations, McHarg employed a sophisticated yet easily understood system entailing (1) an ecological inventory, including studies by experts in hydrology, soils, vegetation, wildlife, and microclimate; (2) interpretation of the ecological data to determine limitations on development; (3) determination of landscape tolerance to man's intrusion; (4) evaluation of land-use programs and their impact on the landscape; and (5) matching of landscape tolerance with land-use needs to delineate areas of development on a gradient of high to low intensity—that is, areas with low-permeable soils and low-quality vegetation lend themselves to high-intensity development, whereas areas with highly permeable soils and high-quality vegetation require low-density development. In this fashion McHarg's system clarified land-use constraints and opportunities which then allowed synthesis into least-cost–greatest-benefit solutions to proposed development.[28]

Application of this system on the basis of data then available led McHarg to accentuate seven goals of land-use programs for the proposed new town:

(1) minimum disruption of the surface and subsurface hydrological regimen;
(2) preservation of the woodland environment;

27. Wallace, McHarg, Roberts and Todd, Woodlands New Community: An Ecological Plan (report prepared for The Woodlands Development Corporation, May, 1974), pp. 2–3, 7. See also Ian McHarg and Jonathan Sutton, "Ecological Plumbing for the Texas Coastal Plain: The Woodlands, New Town Experiment," Landscape Architecture 65 (January, 1975): 78–89.

28. Wallace, McHarg, Roberts and Todd, Woodlands New Community, pp. 6–7, 9–25, 27–30.

(3) establishment of a natural drainage system in floodplains, swales, ponds, and on recharge soils;

(4) preservation of vegetation noted for species diversity, high quality, stability, and uniqueness;

(5) provision of wildlife habitats and movement corridors, so that wildlife now living on the site may remain;

(6) minimization of development cost; and,

(7) avoidance of hazards to life or health.[29]

While McHarg and his associates prepared the ecological inventory and environmental plan, the other consultants set to their respective tasks. Gladstone Associates assembled a three-volume analysis of the economic feasibility of the proposed new community which painted a rosy picture unmarred by few if any somber tones.

There were good reasons for optimism. Existing and projected growth patterns in the five-county Houston Standard Metropolitan Statistical Area (SMSA) placed the project site square in the path of expansion. In the decade 1960–70 metropolitan Houston added 540,000 new residents, a population growth exceeded only by the Anaheim–Santa Ana, California, area and by Washington, D.C. Even more impressive statistics indicated that in the eight-county Houston-Galveston region population tripled from 735,000 to 2,150,000 from 1940 to 1970 and total employment swelled from 285,000 to 857,000, a threefold increase.[30]

Diversification of the Houston economy from the early-day production of raw materials into the manufacture of finished goods and technological research and development activities further brightened the prospects of the new community, for several reasons. First, projected total employment growth exceeded 80 percent, from 857,000 in 1970 to 1,575,000 in 1990. Second, the corresponding expected population increase totaled more than 1 million, from 2 million in 1970 to 3.5 million in 1990. Third, the northwest sector of the Houston SMSA, including southern Montgomery County, was expected to be the main beneficiary of population and economic growth because of its proximity to the 7,000-acre Intercontinental Airport, opened in 1970 after a two-year delay, and because of the availability of land at a reasonable cost. Thus the Gladstone group predicted a rise in the employment base in the northwest sector from 107,000 in 1970 to 380,000 by 1990, population expansion during the same period from 423,000 to

29. Ibid., pp. 29–30.
30. Gladstone Associates, Metropolitan Economic Background, pp. 1, 3.

1,040,000, and a corresponding rise in annual family income and demand for housing.[31]

Translated into projected development in the northwest region, this anticipated economic and population growth meant (1) an increase in demand for single-family residences from 8,100 units annually in the early 1970s to 15,800 units by 1990; (2) a yearly rise in demand for multifamily dwellings from 2,430 units in 1970 to 9,480 by 1990, an increase of almost 300 percent; and (3) added demands by 1990 for 21 million square feet of retail space, 14 million square feet of office space, 7,640 acres of industrial land, and 6,340 hotel and motel rooms. Special advantages enjoyed by The Woodlands site which predicted capture a large share of these increases, included the availability of wooded land, a scarce and desirable commodity in "flat, barren" Houston; an adequate existing and planned highway system; railway transportation; and proximity to the Intercontinental Airport.[32]

The Gladstone plan for the economic development of The Woodlands reflected the group's analysis of employment and population patterns plus considerable input from the other consultants and Mitchell's staff. Basing its recommendations on a five-phase, twenty-year development program, the group proposed construction of a total of 49,000 dwelling units on 6,161 acres with an annual average volume of 435 sale and 165 rental units during phase 1, 1973–75, which would peak at 1,330 sale and 1,950 rental units in phase 4, 1986–90.[33] Proposed housing types and market prices included 800 single-family one-acre "estates" constructed on the "more desirable sites," such as lake and golf-course frontages, selling for an average price of $70,000–$90,000 (this did not preclude the possibility of more pretentious, custom-designed homes costing up to $250,000 if suitably attractive sites were provided); 6,150 detached single-family homes at a density of 3 per acre selling at $30,000 to $50,000; 2,600 patio homes built 6 per acre priced from $25,000 to $40,000; 8,000 townhouses ranging from 4 or 5 up to 15 per acre priced from under $20,000 to over $35,000; 1,300 garden condominiums averaging 12 units per acre priced from $15,000 to over $30,000; and 1,000-plus elevator condominiums at 30 units per acre ranging from $25,000 to $60,000.[34]

Rental housing, which would eventually comprise 50 percent of

31. Ibid., pp. 6, 7, 33, 49, 58.
32. Gladstone Associates, Market Opportunities, pp. 4–6.
33. Gladstone Associates, Development Program, Mitchell-Houston New Community, pp. 2, 17–18. The five-phase development years were 1973–75, 1976–80, 1981–85, 1986–90, and 1991–92.
34. Ibid., pp. 25–28.

the total residential program, also offered a wide range of options: 7,240 townhouses constructed 12 per acre and renting from $200 to $300 a month; more than 8,200 low-density garden apartments built 15 per acre at monthly rentals from $175 to $250; 4,500 high-density garden apartments, 30 per acre, at rents from $150 to $225 a month; and 2,000 elevator apartments, mid-rise to high-rise, constructed 40 per acre, at monthly rentals from $175 to $250 and from $250 to $500, respectively.[35]

Of the total 49,000 residential units, 7,300, or 15 percent, would be assisted housing for low- and moderate-income families consisting of owner-occupied single-family units and garden and elevator apartments. Also, because of the comparatively low housing prices in the Houston area, the Gladstone group expected that enough low-priced unassisted housing would be available to increase the number of low- and moderate-income residences to 30 percent of the total. To avoid clustering of low- and moderate-income housing and the attendant social stigma, they proposed that the residences differ little in physical appearance and that they be scattered at random throughout the site.[36]

The Gladstone group furthermore proposed that, because of local and national trends, changes in life-styles, and growing public acceptance of high-density land use, The Woodlands offer an ever-escalating number of townhouses, garden and elevator condominiums, and patio homes. While the inclusion in the development program of an increasingly larger increment of high-density housing admittedly represented "the major risk element," the Gladstone group was convinced that "the level of preservicing . . . , the prime location of the site in the rapidly developing northwest sector, and the natural tree cover of the property . . . , all serve to enhance the project's marketability and allow for a greater degree of innovation."[37]

The services-and-amenities package proposed by Gladstone, again with input from the other consultants and Mitchell's staff, took its cue from the experience of other new towns, especially Columbia, Maryland. Columbia's design emphasized the clustering of neighborhoods and villages around a central or downtown core, a large percentage of open space, bicycle and pedestrian paths, and village recreation centers and elementary schools within walking distance of each neighborhood.[38] The Gladstone plan for The Woodlands thus included vil-

35. Ibid., pp. 28–29.
36. Ibid., pp. 19–21, 30.
37. Ibid., pp. 21–24, 34.
38. "Privately Financed New Communities," *Architectural Record* 154 (December, 1973): 108–109.

lage recreation areas in each of the planned six villages and in the university center at a capital cost of $1 million per center and an annual operating expenditure of $100,000; a recreation center in each of the nineteen neighborhoods at a capital expenditure of $200,000 each and yearly operating expenses of $20,000; seven nursery day-care centers, one in each village and in the university center, at a capital cost of $250,000 each and an annual subsidy of $25,000 each for operating costs; seven early-learning centers for preschool children at a cost of $100,000 each and $10,000 annually to subsidize operations; two public golf courses costing $400,000 apiece; three horseback riding stables at $50,000 each; ninety-five "tot lots" (children's playgrounds) at $5,000 each and $100 annually for maintenance and repair; an outdoor theater and other unspecified cultural facilities at a cost of $575,000 ($75,000 for the theater) and an annual operating budget of $50,000; and a community-wide pathway system at a cost of $30,000 per segment and $2,600 a year for repair, maintenance, and lighting.[39]

Although not spelled out in detail, the amenities-and-services program would be administered by a community association and funded through an annual assessment levied on residential, commercial, and industrial owners. While the program was expected to become self-sustaining eventually, debt financing through 1986 in the amount of $11 million would have to be borne by the developer.[40]

The Gladstone group concluded its report with a projected cash-flow analysis which, like other statistics, gave cause for optimism. Heavy initial development costs, including the amenities-and-services package, required $30,334,000 of developer investment or negative cash flow through 1973. Projected total development costs over the twenty-year program, excluding interest and income tax payments, amounted to $140 million, while projected revenues totaled $690 million, for a net cash flow of $550 million. These projections, and the calculated rate of return on investment of 23.5 percent, led the Gladstone group to observe that "such an investment yield from land development activities is highly attractive in its own right, and when combined with other potential profits from associated building and ownership opportunities on the new community site, establishes this proposed new town as a superior land development investment." In fact, they added, because of the regional economy's vigorous growth and the location of the site athwart metropolitan expansion "the risk associated with this land development venture is felt to be only moderate, and *there is sub-*

39. Gladstone Associates, Development Program, pp. 76–78.
40. Ibid., pp. 80, 84.

stantial opportunity for bettering . . . development projections through superior management of the project, if regional economic growth continues as vigorously as in the past decade." [Italics added][41]

Not surprisingly, institutional and social planning, which began in November, 1970, progressed more slowly and with greater uncertainty than either the environmental or the economic program. Even the selection of a name for the new community caused considerable quandary. In keeping with the agreed-upon need to feature the forest as the major asset of the new town, suggested names included Cross Timbers, Glen Eden, Woodstock, and Woodlands. Some members of the planning team for a time favored Woodstock because it was well known and hence provided instant recognition; it had "wood" in the name and was a single word. On the other hand, Woodstock was associated with revolution and drugs—the former might be turned to good use because the new town intended to be "revolutionary" in many ways, but the negative connotations, drugs or narcotics, could not be easily overcome. So persuaded, in the end the group opted for "The Woodlands," a name suggested by Mitchell's wife, Cynthia, and one which possessed all of the desirable mental associations and none of the negative ones.[42]

As early as 1969 and the Ross plan for a new town, George Mitchell deemed a university campus to be essential to his maturing conception of a self-sustained community. Discussions in planning-team meetings confirmed and buttressed his conviction, and on January 4, 1971, Mitchell took President Philip G. Hoffman and Vice-President Coulson Tough of the University of Houston on a tour of the site of the new town. On the following day, after a visual presentation to the university's board of regents, Mitchell formally offered the university a gift of 350 acres with an option to purchase an additional 100 acres for a north-branch campus.[43] Three months later Hoffman informed Mitchell that the board of regents had accepted the offer "in principle" and subject to clarification of the exact campus site, cost of the 100 optional acres, and assurance of adequate utilities. Thus advised, and to make the offer more enticing to the regents, on May 6, 1971, Mitchell proposed a 400-acre donation without a purchase option, final determination of the campus location to be mutually agreed upon. Nearly a year later, on March 7, 1972, the regents accepted Mitchell's altered

41. Ibid., pp. 4–5, 7, 98.
42. "Woodlands Village Chronicle (manuscript in WDC Papers), March 11–12, 1971; October 16–17, 1971; "The Woodlands Chronicle," p. 25.
43. "The Woodlands Village Chronicle," January 5, 1971.

39

Members of the University of Houston's Board of Regents and C. F. McIlhenney, university vice-president, on a tour of The Woodlands site, 1971. Left to right: Mrs. Gus Wortham, Robert Hartsfield, McIlhenney, and A. J. Farfel.

proposal.[44] It now remained to obtain authorization from the Texas State Coordinating Board for a north-branch campus, but for the moment at least The Woodlands was to have its university.

While many members of the planning team and Mitchell's staff at times bubbled over in their enthusiasm and commitment to innovative social and institutional planning, few possessed expertise in sociology, psychology, public health, and other relevant academic disciplines. Mitchell proved, however, as he usually did, to be imaginative and resourceful in tapping external sources. In February, 1971, three members of the University of Texas School of Public Health, including Charles

40   44. "The Woodlands Chronicle," pp. 18–19, 29, 31, 50–51.

Planning session, 1971. Front, left to right: *James Veltman, Ian McHarg, Robert Hartsfield.* Back, left to right: *R. E. Clark and Morris Thompson, vice-presidents of Mitchell Energy and Development Corporation.*

Kelly, a doctoral candidate who subsequently became Mitchell's director of social and institutional planning, joined the planning team as consultants.[45] Several months later, in October, 1971, Mitchell invited a group of nationally eminent social and behavioral scientists, educators, and public health specialists to join his staff and consultants in a two-day seminar to discuss the relationship of physical structure to institutional and human behavior and methods of institutional planning.[46] Although the seminar did not produce any structural conceptualization, the interplay of ideas provided a catalyst for much of the

45. Ibid., p. 21; interview with Charles Kelly, August 31, 1982.
46. "Woodlands Village Chronicle," October 16–17, 1971.

Planning session, 1971. Front, left to right: *George P. Mitchell and William Pereira.*

social and institutional design incorporated in the development plan. As one of the participants later observed, "The entire planning process has to maintain a delicate balance between the particular and the general, the individual pieces of the puzzle and the overall picture. This means many working groups that are integrated only after each has done its homework. Do I think it can be done in the 1970's? Yes, but like porcupines mating: v-e-r-y carefully."[47]

From the outset of the project Mitchell placed high priority on planning for institutional religion in The Woodlands. He became convinced early in the planning process of the efficacy of the Columbia model, which avoided traditional denominational exclusiveness in the form of separate buildings and unilateral community interaction in favor of

42   47. Undated letter from Yehudi A. Cohen to David Hendricks, quoted in ibid.

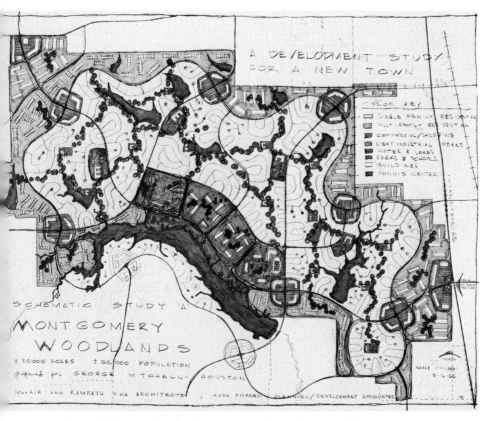

First plan of The Woodlands, drawn in 1966 by architect Karl Kamrath.

shared facilities and multilateral community involvement. Such innovation, Mitchell believed, served two purposes: economy in land use
and an enhancement of the desired sense of community. In June, 1971,
after discussions with his minister, the Reverend G. Richard Wheat-
croft, Mitchell invited a group of representative religious leaders, Jews,
Roman Catholics, and Protestants, in the Houston area to meet with
David Hendricks and other members of his staff. After preliminary discussions the group organized itself as the Religious Institutions Planning group and on February 10, 1972, adopted a statement, "Towards
an Interfaith Covenant," in which they affirmed their support of cooperative planning, a cooperative ministry, and cooperative community
service.[48]

48. "The Woodlands Chronicle," pp. 35–36; Alvin H. Franzmeier and Donald R.   **43**

In the midst of this spate of planning, a formal presentation of plans for the new town was presented to HUD on March 31, 1971. Several months later HUD informed the Mitchell group that the New Community Development Corporation (NCDC) would probably review The Woodlands application in September, and on August 10, 1971, Mitchell submitted a developmental master plan. Although HUD officials described the application as the "strongest and best" yet received, in late October difficulties arose when the federal agency questioned the projected figures for low- and moderate-income housing, financing, and some aspects of general planning and engineering. HUD's questioning provoked some talk in Mitchell's group of abandoning HUD and seeking private financing—a course not seriously considered by Mitchell—and on November 23, 1971, after Mitchell submitted a revised financial and cash-flow analysis, the NCDC gave tentative approval to The Woodlands application.[49]

Gebert, *The Woodlands Experience: An Unfinished History of the Interfaith Movement in a New Town in Texas,* pp. 4–7.

49. "Woodlands Village Chronicle," March 31, 1971; "The Woodlands Chronicle," pp. 35, 39–40, 47, 49.

4. Birth of a New Town, 1971–1974

Tentative approval by HUD of The Woodlands application in November, 1971, capped over twelve months of constant, and for the most part successful, activity by Mitchell's staff. In addition to coordinating planning, the hardworking group confronted a series of difficulties provoked by local authorities and by public concern about the impact of a new town on life-style and property values in southern Montgomery County.

In addition to other requirements, HUD made approval of an application conditional on prior sanction (known as "A-95 clearance") by a local entity, or entities, upon which a new town might have an impact — in this instance the Houston-Galveston Area Council (HGAC) and the cities of Conroe and Houston.[1] Although no public announcement had been made by October, 1971, of Mitchell's plans or of the application to HUD, his staff had informed local government bodies and various public officials about his intentions. In fact, as early as April, 1971, Gerard H. Coleman, executive director of the HGAC, attended a Mitchell staff planning session.[2] Earlier, in February, 1971, Mitchell and four staff members had met with part owner Owens Rigby and reporter

---

1. "A-95 clearance" takes its name from a circular of that number issued by the U.S. Office of Management and Budget in accordance with the Intergovernmental Cooperation Act of 1968. While notification of local governing bodies is required, resolution of criticisms is not. H. Carter McFarland, *Federal Government and Urban Problems: HUD — Successes, Failures, and the Fate of Our Cities*, p. 61.

2. "The Woodlands Chronicle," (manuscript in WDC papers), p. 29.

Thomas Bacon of the *Conroe Courier*. During the meeting Mitchell gave them a detailed oral description of the new-town project and asked them not to air his plans until financing arrangements had been completed with HUD.[3]

The *Courier* honored his request for public silence until October 3, 1971, when the newspaper reported an impending public meeting on October 5 of the HGAC at which Mitchell Energy and Development Corporation intended to seek approval of a new community in southern Montgomery County. This announcement, plus subsequent reports by the *Courier,* the *Houston Post,* and the *Houston Chronicle* on October 6 about the new-community project and the approval of the proposal by the HGAC's project-review committee, forced Mitchell's staff on the same day prematurely to petition the City of Houston to extend its extraterritorial jurisdiction to cover The Woodlands site.[4] Such action by Houston would serve several purposes: the site could not be annexed by another city; future residents of The Woodlands could not incorporate without Houston's permission, and Houston logically would not choose to annex the area for at least twenty-five years because of the new town's bonded indebtedness and tax base, thus leaving Mitchell in near-absolute control during the development period.

While Mitchell's staff agreed on the desirability of extraterritorial jurisdiction by Houston, the petition and the publicity given to the new town produced cries of outrage in Conroe and Montgomery County and obstructive maneuvers by the Conroe City Council, the Montgomery County Planning Commission, and the Montgomery County Commissioners' Court. Robert H. Buchanan, a consulting engineer and acting Montgomery County engineer as well as chairman of the Montgomery County Planning Commission, claimed previous ignorance of the project, an assertion denied by members of Mitchell's staff. Buchanan quickly assumed leadership of the opposition.[5] After a meeting of the Montgomery County Planning Commission on Octo-

3. "Woodlands Village Chronicle," (manuscript in WDC papers), February 22, 1971.

4. Ibid., November 12, 1971; *Houston Post,* October 6, 7, 1971. The *Post* reported that the HGAC review committee had "enthusiastically" approved the project and characterized the committee as "most impressed with the detail, the concept, the degree of time, research, energy, and talent Mitchell has brought to the project."

5. Comments by these public officials support the Mitchell group's denial. Gerard Coleman informed HUD, "It has been the experience of our staff that the Mitchell firm has been more thorough than most in its own efforts to consult and cooperate with both local government and with State and Federal technical personnel." Gerard Coleman to Ann Hilliard, November 19, 1971, WDC Papers. An officer in the U.S. Soil Conservation Service stated that his office had been informed of the project in February

ber 7, Buchanan informed the HGAC of the commission's "surprise" that Mitchell planned a new town in the county, complained that despite the project's magnitude Mitchell had failed to submit the plans to them, and warned that because of this omission "we will have no recourse other than to ask the Commissioners' Court to pass a resolution denying this grant."[6]

To counter mounting opposition, Mitchell's staff quickly arranged meetings with Buchanan, the Conroe City Council, the Montgomery County Planning Commission, the Montgomery County Commissioners' Court, Conroe Mayor Mickey Deison, and County Judge Lynn Coker.

The sessions resulted in expressions of support for the new community (except from Buchanan, who remained adamant in opposition), but emphatic disapproval of the petition to Houston for extension of extraterritorial jurisdiction. Residents of the area, especially those in neighboring Oak Ridge North, also expressed fears that the presence of the Houston colossus meant the introduction of its problems as well — pollution, crime, taxes, poor schools, traffic congestion, and too many people. Once the meaning of extraterritorial jurisdiction was explained to them, most of the residents departed at least mollified, if not enthusiastic.[7] At a meeting on October 13, from which Buchanan was absent, the Montgomery County Planning Commission voted to rescind its previous letter of opposition and to so inform the commissioners' court. The court, after rejecting a request by Buchanan to approve a resolution opposing any further encroachment by Houston, withdrew all previous objections made by the planning commission and Montgomery County, approved the new-town project, and asked the HGAC to follow suit.[8]

The HGAC's executive committee then presented the final hurdle, at least in terms of obtaining A-95 clearance. At the committee meeting on October 19 the still-unresolved question of extraterritorial jurisdiction again intruded to further muddy the waters. Several members of the council argued that action should be tabled pending Houston's decision. After Mitchell and his staff explained that A-95 clearance and

and added, "Our office has been favorably impressed at the amount of preplanning that has gone into this project before actual construction of the new city begins." Norman O. Wilson to William Ainley, November 17, 1971, WDC Papers.

6. Robert H. Buchanan to Houston-Galveston Area Council, October 7, 1971, WDC Papers.

7. "Woodlands Village Chronicle," November 12, 1971.

8. Resolution of Montgomery County Commissioners' Court, October 15, 1971, WDC Papers.

extraterritorial jurisdiction were separate and unrelated issues, the members approved the project 11 to 0 with 3 abstentions.[9]

On the following day, despite some apprehension among Mitchell's staff members, the Houston City Council dealt expeditiously with the matter of extraterritorial jurisdiction. After a cursory discussion lasting less than one minute, the council unanimously approved the petition.[10]

HUD's tentative approval of the project plan also prompted a reorganization of Mitchell's planning staff, the hiring of more consultants, and the addition of key executive personnel. A crucial earlier appointment in September, 1971, had brought J. Leonard (Len) Ivins into the Mitchell organization from Columbia, Maryland, where he had served as vice-president and director of development. In his new positions as senior vice-president in charge of real estate, as a member of the Board of Directors of Mitchell Energy and Development Corporation, and as president of The Woodlands Development Corporation after its formation in July, 1972, Ivins bore direct responsibility second only to that of George Mitchell for implementation of the planning design for The Woodlands.[11]

Ivins's appointment was unquestionably helpful in the subsequent luring away from Columbia of several of his former associates between December, 1971, and February, 1972. Those individuals included Ralph Everhart, who became senior project manager of land development; Robert Grace, who assumed the position of vice-president and director of land development; Jack Price, who became project manager of utilities; and Ben F. Worley, who took over as development director of the yet-to-be-formed Woodlands Community Association. To this group of former Rouse Company employees was added, in July, 1972, Salvatore T. ("Sam") Calleri, formerly chief financial officer of Howard Research and Development Corporation (a subsidiary of the Rouse Company). Calleri was named vice-president of finance for Mitchell Energy and Development Corporation and The Woodlands Development Corporation.[12]

In concurrent reorganization of the planning staff David Hendricks

9. "Woodlands Village Chronicle," November 12, 1971. Gerard Coleman resigned as executive director of HGAC in January, 1973, to accept a position as vice-president, governmental affairs, with Mitchell Energy and Development Corporation. He suffered a heart attack and died in March, 1974. *Houston Chronicle,* January 26, 1973; ibid., March 19, 1974.

10. "Woodlands Village Chronicle," November 12, 1971.

11. *Woodlands Newsletter,* March–April, 1973, p. 5.

12. Ibid., August–September, 1973, p. 4; October–November, 1973, pp. 4, 6.

was moved from manager of institutional development to assistant general manager of The Woodlands; Robert Hartsfield became director of residential development; James Veltman took over Hartsfield's former position as director of environmental planning and design; and Charles Kelly, a consultant since early 1971, became manager of institutional development.[13] This combination of executive managers and second-tier planners guided The Woodlands through its first two years. The group, with the aid of a cadre of additional consultants, also began implementing the development plan on which HUD based its commitment in April, 1972, and which was embodied in the Project Agreement signed by HUD and The Woodlands Development Corporation on August 23, 1972.

Under the Project Agreement, HUD guaranteed $50 million in debentures. On September 6, 1972, The Woodlands Development Corporation completed the sale of the debentures to private investors at an interest rate of 7.1 percent. In return HUD required Mitchell to raise the company's equity to $10 million and pay HUD a fee of $170,000. The Woodlands Development Corporation pledged to develop The Woodlands in accordance with its previously submitted development plan and to "use its good efforts" to achieve the goals outlined by the 1970 Urban Growth and New Communities Act, including the provision of low- and moderate-income housing.[14]

In general terms The Woodlands Development Corporation agreed to provide "all of the basic activities and facilities normally associated with a city or town, including housing, employment, education, culture, health, transportation, commerce, industry, social services, and recreation in a balanced and harmonious whole, so as to be economically sound and create an attractive environment in which to live, work, and play."[15]

In more specific terms the twenty-year development plan projected a community of 150,000 persons on 16,973 acres, 3,909 acres, or 23 percent, of which would be maintained as open space with ample parks, pathways, equestrian trails, lakes, golf courses, and other amenities. The plan also provided for two centers—a Metro Center and a University or Town Center—plus seven residential villages composed of clusters and neighborhoods built around elementary schools and containing

13. "The Woodlands Chronicle," p. 50.

14. Project Agreement between the United States of America and The Woodlands Development Corporation, August 23, 1972, pp. 1, 24–31; hereafter cited as Project Agreement.

15. The Woodlands Development Corporation Development Plan, exhibits G, G-4; hereafter cited as Development Plan.

The Woodlands

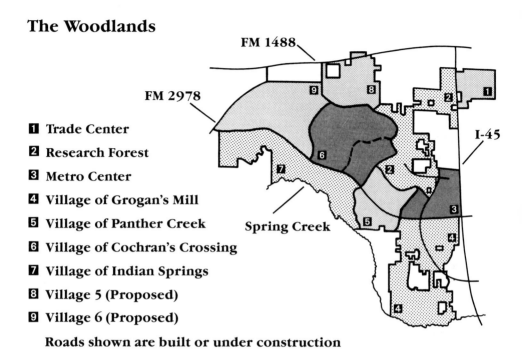

FM 1488

FM 2978

I-45

1 **Trade Center**

2 **Research Forest**

3 **Metro Center**

4 **Village of Grogan's Mill**

5 **Village of Panther Creek**   **Spring Creek**

6 **Village of Cochran's Crossing**

7 **Village of Indian Springs**

8 **Village 5 (Proposed)**

9 **Village 6 (Proposed)**

Roads shown are built or under construction

Map of the village design of The Woodlands and major arterials.

various recreational facilities as well as convenience shopping malls. Within this geographical scheme The Woodlands Development Corporation projected the construction of 12,495 single-family detached units, 14,830 single-family attached units, and 20,050 multiple-family units—a total of 47,375 residences with a combined average density of 7.5 units per square acre. These totals included 12,938 units for low- and moderate-income families.[16]

In keeping with its emphasis on innovation and ethnic-economic mix, the plan required a broad range of housing designs and prices with low- and moderate-income housing widely distributed throughout the project. To further ensure integration and preclude stigmatization, such housing was to be relatively indistinguishable in terms of architectural style and quality.[17]

16. Ibid., exhibits G5–G7, G27.

17. Ibid., exhibits G5, G7. Heterogeneous as opposed to homogeneous neighborhoods in terms of home-price ranges also emulated Columbia. Herbert Gans, who served as a consultant at Columbia, had unsuccessfully argued against heterogeneous grouping because people prefer homogeneous neighborhoods. He also predicted with some

50

To enhance town, neighborhood, and village cohesiveness and sense of community, all the entities were to contain various commercial, cultural, recreational, and educational facilities. Thus the Metro Center would serve retail, office, entertainment, hotel, and restricted industrial uses, while the Town or University Center would provide facilities oriented toward community cultural and institutional activities. Planning for each village and neighborhood center contemplated less elaborate commercial establishments at each level and included a common recreational facility—normally tennis courts or a swimming pool —plus either an elementary or a secondary school to which the center related.[18]

To provide diverse employment opportunities for residents, the development plan projected two thousand acres of industrial parks and required the developer to construct, or cause to be constructed, storm-drainage, water, and sewer facilities as well as a road system designed to permit easy egress and ingress to and from residential and industrial-park areas. In the same context the developer also pledged to provide a "structured" road network including expressways, collector and loop streets, cul-de-sacs, bicycle paths, and pedestrian walkways coordinated in a fashion to permit safe and convenient movement throughout the project.[19]

A major portion of the development plan dealt with environmental concerns and stipulated that "a high quality physical environment including natural features, structures, landscaping, open space and recreational areas will be preserved, created and maintained. Procedures and techniques for land planning, land development, and construction will be established to preserve and enhance the natural surroundings and create a healthful, ecologically sound, and aesthetically pleasing community." To attain these goals, the developer would make every effort to preserve existing tree cover and ground vegetation essential to the control of erosion and sedimentation. The developer would also provide storm-drainage and water-treatment systems capable of preventing unacceptable levels of pollution of Lake Houston, its tributaries, and surrounding floodplains. Finally, the water-management system should eliminate the potential danger of flash floods and minimize the impact of development on the hydrologic cycle.[20]

---

accuracy that mixed grouping would cause social problems in Columbia. Frederick Steiner, The Politics of New Town Planning: The Newfields, Ohio, Story, p. 220.

18. The Woodlands Development Corporation, Development Plan, exhibits G15, G17.

19. Ibid., exhibits G17–G21.

20. Ibid., exhibits G22–G28.

51

Other articles in the development plan provided for (1) public utilities, placed underground whenever practicable, including telephone, electric, gas, sewer, and water systems as well as solid-waste collection and cable-television service; (2) a comprehensive health-care program; (3) a full range of educational facilities and instruction ranging from child-learning and day-care centers to elementary and secondary schools, adult-education and business-training seminars, and university courses (the mature system contemplated twenty elementary schools, six middle schools, six junior high schools, and three high schools plus a four-hundred-acre University of Houston campus); (4) cultural facilities including outdoor sculpture, open-air theaters, art galleries, music auditoriums, and exhibit halls; (5) the establishment of quasi-government organizations and community associations to enable resident participation in decision making. To these ends the developer would establish continuing communication with the residents including, but not limited to, orientation meetings, planning sessions, and a monthly newsletter. Also, residents would be briefed on development plans at least semiannually, and their ideas would be incorporated into the program when feasible.[21]

The Project Agreement recognized that changing economic, employment, and financial patterns and other factors might require periodic amendment of the development plan. It also stipulated, however, that any substantial change, defined as one which affected achievement of the goals of the 1970 legislation, required prior approval by HUD.[22]

After HUD made its commitment in April, 1972, planning and infrastructure construction assumed a feverish pace in preparation for the first village, embracing 1,750 acres, to be named Grogan's Mill, and a 135-acre industrial park. While directing the heightened planning and construction activity, Len Ivins also presided over a number of management decisions which had long-term, and in some instances deleterious, consequences for The Woodlands. His previous experience in Columbia from 1965 until his departure in early fall, 1971, unquestionably influenced Ivins to duplicate the example set by James Rouse and particularly his large financial expenditures for consumer-attractive development before opening the project. Sometimes referred to as the "gem" of the new towns and "the next America," Columbia enjoyed spectacular success from the beginning of its development in 1965 until the full impact of the economic recession became apparent

21. Ibid., exhibits G29–G41.
22. Project Agreement, p. 49.

in early 1975. Within three years of breaking ground, construction on the nearly 14,000-acre site included a town center with a completed eight-story office building overlooking a 32-acre man-made lake, another office building in progress, a second man-made lake, a $1 million music pavilion, and preliminary preparations for an enclosed shopping mall which when completed in 1972 accommodated two department stores and 102 retail outlets. By the end of 1972, Columbia boasted a population of approximately 24,000, one completed village, and five villages under way. Total investment in the project through December, 1973, had reached nearly $100 million.[23]

Impressed by Rouse's success in Columbia, Ivins persuaded The Woodlands Development Corporation to invest large amounts of capital in "massive" non–Title VII activity, including the construction of a 335-acre Commercial, Conference, and Leisure Center (CCLC) with extensive shopping, commercial, office, and recreational facilities. Construction also began on the 200-room Woodlands Inn, an eighteen-hole golf course, and an Information Center plus excavation of a 15-acre lake as part of the CCLC's amenity package. This decision in turn necessitated an increased tempo as well as a proliferation of road construction, including interchanges on I-45, to ease access to the building sites and for marketing purposes. While ultimately necessary, heavy road construction added further to swelling expenditures, as did a concurrent ballooning of The Woodlands Development Corporation staff to 365 persons, 65 of whom earned annual salaries in excess of $30,000.[24]

Other factors not necessarily controllable by management added to initial problems. Heavy rains during the spring of 1973 slowed construction to the point that expected completion dates lagged five months

23. *Central Maryland News,* August 19, 1971; Hoyt Gimlin, "New Towns," in William B. Dickinson, Jr., ed., *Editorial Research Reports on the Urban Environment,* pp. 168–69; "Privately Financed New Communities," *Architectural Record* 154 (December, 1973): 108–109; Richard O. Brooks, *New Towns and Communal Values: A Case Study of Columbia, Maryland,* p. 8. Construction began in June, 1966. By that time planning costs amounted to $3 million, and land purchases totaled $25 million. More than $50 million had been spent by June 21, 1967, when dedication ceremonies formally opened the new town. Gurney Breckenfeld, *Columbia and the New Cities,* pp. 276–77. Rouse obtained capital from Connecticut General Life Insurance Company, Teachers Insurance and Annuity Association, and Chase Manhattan Bank. Columbia's fortunes peaked in 1971–73 and fell rapidly thereafter. Annual land sales averaged $24 million in 1971, 1972, and 1973 but plunged to $6.5 million in 1974. *Washington Post,* January 13, 1975; "Can 'New Towns' Survive the Economic Crunch?" *Business Week* 2367 (February 10, 1975): 43–44.

24. Booz-Allen and Hamilton, Inc., *New Communities: Problems and Potentials,* Appendix C, "An Assessment of the Causes of Current Problems, Case Study H: Woodlands," H-I-3, H-II-4, H-III-1, H-VIII-1, H-VIII-2, H-VIII-9.

Woodlands Parkway under construction.

or more behind schedule. HUD also contributed to the difficulties by refusing to approve deed covenants submitted in January, 1973, by The Woodlands Development Corporation until January, 1974, because of questions regarding the intended role of The Woodlands Community Association in financing recreational amenities. Financing could not be obtained in the interim, and, equally serious, land sales could not be completed – a hiatus which meant that expected and sorely needed revenues did not materialize. HUD further added to The Woodlands' financial difficulties by failing, for a number of reasons, to provide supplementary grants authorized by the 1970 legislation for special planning and for installation of sewer, water, and drainage systems.[25]

Nonetheless, by the end of October, 1973, a HUD investigator de-

54   25. Ibid., H-III-8.

Woodlands Parkway, 1986.

scribed activity on the site as "impressive." He particularly noted on-going construction of the CCLC, started in July, 1973, the partial completion of an office building, and the start of the first units of condominiums, townhouses, and apartments adjacent to the CCLC. The investigator predicted that by spring, 1974, The Woodlands would be a "showplace."[26]

Less discernible but equally vital activity included the establishment of two municipal utilities districts (MUDs) which under Texas law assume a quasi-government character for the purpose of providing water and sewer services. At the same time planners began developing a unique natural-drainage system in keeping with Ian McHarg's ecological inventory and its emphasis on the hydrologic cycle. To implement

26. Ibid., H-III-9.

The Wharf, Lake Harrison, and the golf course under construction.

McHarg's recommendations, and to develop a twenty-year master plan for water, sewer, and drainage facilities, in March, 1972, The Woodlands Development Corporation retained the firm of Turner, Collie and Braden, Inc., Consulting Engineers. Using data provided by McHarg's studies and additional input from land designers, thoroughfare planners, geotechnical engineers, groundwater hydrologists, and the U.S. Soil Conservation Service, the engineers devised a natural-drainage system utilizing shallow grass swales, retention ponds and lakes, greenbelt corridors, golf-course fairways, porous pavement for roads and parking areas, and even curbless streets, which not only maximized the preservation of the natural beauty of The Woodlands but also saved an estimated $14,478,900 of the cost of a conventional system.

The sewage system designed by the consulting engineers consisted **56** of three treatment plants, the first to be located on Panther Branch to

The Wharf, Lake Harrison, and the golf course after completion.

serve the first village. It employed conventional treatment processes and would have an eventual capacity of 6 million gallons a day. The plan also contemplated discharging part of the treated effluent into streams and lakes and using a portion to irrigate golf courses and other areas. Turner, Collie and Braden estimated the cost of sewage facilities at $4,600,000 for the initial development and $39,250,000 for the entire project.

The water-supply system for Grogan's Mill Village required the initial drilling of six wells plus an additional thirty-three for the mature system. The estimated cost of the facilities, including pump stations, distribution mains, storage tanks, and miscellaneous equipment, amounted to $3,037,000 for phase 1 and $26,256,000 for the project.[27]

27. Turner, Collie and Braden, Inc., A Case History of The Woodlands—A Project

When initial construction began in The Woodlands on September 29, 1972, with the ritual accompanying the removal of the first tree on the site, one permanent structure, Lamar Elementary School, built by Conroe Independent School District in 1971, broke the otherwise undisturbed expanse of forest, grassland, and wandering creeks. A temporary road connecting the school to an overpass across I-45 provided sole access into the tract, and a gravel logging road which meandered through the woods was the only avenue to construction sites. Heavy rains and even a rare snowfall plus the passage of heavy trucks turned these already inadequate conduits into seas of mud which defied transit by vehicles of any description.

Despite these physical difficulties, in mid-January, 1973, George Mitchell announced that construction would begin within the next few weeks on a $12 million CCLC including a two-hundred-room inn and conference center with seventeen meeting or seminar rooms and three indoor tennis courts that could be converted into conference, banquet, and exhibit space; a country club with two eighteen-hole golf courses complete with dining and lounging facilities; an Olympic-size swimming pool and health studios containing saunas, steam rooms, exercise areas, and locker space; an equestrian center; an indoor ice-skating rink; a seventeen-acre lake; three hundred single- and multifamily housing units; and an enclosed shopping mall connecting The Woodlands Inn and Country Club with the first village center of Grogan's Mill. By midsummer, however, construction other than infrastructure had been limited to groundbreaking exercises for the first of two buildings in the Office Park and the start of two townhouse clusters in Grogan's Mill Village.[28]

While the beginning of residential construction conformed to long-range development plans, the decision to build two townhouse clusters also served an immediate utilitarian purpose. Texas laws adopted early in the twentieth century and in 1971 provided for the creation of drainage and municipal utility districts through petition by registered voters and/or landowners within a described area. The statutes also empowered legally constituted district authorities to hold bond issues, which (subject to voter approval) would defray the costs of water, sewer, and drainage systems. Creation of such districts within The Woodlands ob-

of The Woodlands Development Corporation: Land Development Engineering for a "New Town," 5–12.

28. *Conroe Daily Courier*, January 11, 1973, January 14, 1973, March 10, 1974; *Houston Chronicle*, January 11, 1973; The Woodlands Development Corporation, news release, May 6, 1981.

viously would result in reimbursement to the developer for expenditures for those systems. On March 21, 1974, following state approval of MUD No. 6, embracing 1,364 acres within The Woodlands, eighteen registered voters owning townhouses in the new town unanimously approved a $20,750,000 bond issue, 60 percent of which would defray immediate expenditures.[29]

Only ten days earlier, on March 11, the Montgomery County Commissioners' Court had voted preliminary approval of the creation of Drainage District No. 2, embracing about 5,500 acres in The Woodlands, and called for a bond issue of $7,831,999 – $3 million of which would be spent for nonconstruction purposes including engineering fees, investigative research, land acquisition, and land clearing. The court also heard from representatives of Turner, Collie and Braden, the engineering firm employed by The Woodlands Development Corporation, and from a member of Vinson and Elkins, a Houston-based legal firm providing counsel to the corporation. The attorney urged the commissioners' court to approve the employment of Turner, Collie and Braden to review its proposed drainage system, the next step preliminary to a bond election. Although Judge Lynn Coker questioned the propriety of hiring the engineering firm which had devised the plan to review its own work and subsequently cast the lone dissenting vote, the commissioners' court approved both the creation of the district and the employment of Turner, Collie and Braden.[30]

On May 6, 1974, the creation of Drainage District No. 2 received the unanimous approval of the commissioners' court, as did Turner, Collie and Braden's review of its own engineering plan. The proposed system called for construction of three retention ponds, three swales, and three drainage ditches, including a ditch paralleling the west side of I-45 and running south from The Woodlands' northern boundary to Spring Creek, the new town's southern boundary. When residents of neighboring Oak Ridge North voiced concern that the result would be increased dumping of water into Spring Creek and consequent flooding of their homes, representatives of Turner, Collie and Braden assured them that this system would prevent sheeting from west to east across I-45 and would decrease the streamflow, minimizing the threat of high water. One month later, on June 5, 1974, registered vot-

29. *Vernon's Texas Codes Annotated* (1972), II, 274–344, 542–620; *Conroe Daily Courier,* March 24, 1974. The *Courier* also pointed out that eleven townhouses had been sold, most of them to employees of the corporation, in anticipation of a bond-issue election. *Conroe Daily Courier,* March 10, 1974.

30. *Conroe Daily Courier,* March 11, March 14, 1974.

ers in The Woodlands approved a bond issue of $7,831,000 by a vote of 13 to 2.[31]

Approval of utility and drainage district bonds, while they ensured ultimate reimbursement of water, sewer, and drainage expenditures to the financially pressed developer, did not terminate difficulties arising from hydrologic problems. As early as October, 1973, homeowners in Oak Ridge North and that community's developer, Dean Couch, of Associated Properties, complained that their development had flooded three times during the year and pointed an accusatory finger at construction activity in The Woodlands. In August, 1974, following creation of the drainage district, Couch complained to the commissioners' court that The Woodlands Development Corporation officers had informed him that the company wished to postpone installation of proposed drainage facilities north of Robinson Road for as long as ten years because The Woodlands did not need them. Despite assurances from Len Ivins to the contrary and affirmation from the directors of MUD No. 2 that they intended to pursue original plans, suspicions about The Woodlands Development Corporation's intentions persisted. Following a report by engineers employed by Oak Ridge North MUD which attributed 16.25 percent of the water flow into Oak Ridge North's drainage system to runoff from The Woodlands, the district's board of directors asked for a financial contribution from The Woodlands Development Corporation. After a delay of several weeks Robinson G. Lapp, the company's director of community operations, responded that the first priority of Drainage District No. 2 would be installation of a ditch running south from Woodlands Parkway (Robinson Road) on the west side of I-45 to a point immediately above the confluence of Panther and Spring creeks. The district also intended, Lapp wrote, to install berms and channels north of the parkway to create a system which "will eliminate virtually all of the runoff water" flowing over or under the interstate highway. Lapp's assurances, plus a subsequent abatement of flooding in Oak Ridge North, sufficed to still complaints from that quarter, but they arose again in quite a different vein during the summer of 1976.[32]

In the meantime, construction in The Woodlands accelerated in hopes of meeting a rescheduled August, 1974, opening date. On January 27, Robert W. McGee, vice-president and general manager of The

31. Ibid., March 24, May 6, June 6, 1974.
32. *Houston Post,* October 4, 1973; *Conroe Daily Courier,* August 6, October 24, November 21, November 27, December 19, 1974.

Woodlands Development Corporation, announced the impending opening of the new town later in the year with some $68 million in improvements either completed or in progress. Construction in Grogan's Mill Village included grading and graveling of twenty-four miles of roads, installation of water and sewer systems, clearing and grading of an eighteen-hole golf course, lake excavations, and construction of the inn and country club, the conference center, office buildings, and two schools. On January 31, 1974, the first residents of The Woodlands, the Ralph Everhart family, occupied their completed townhouse, and were joined shortly thereafter by ten more families. By the end of February seven Houston-area residential home builders had concluded contracts with The Woodlands Development Corporation providing for approximately $3 million in land purchases, and Mitchell Energy and Development Corporation, or its subsidiaries, had contracted for an additional $4 million. One month later the installation of ten miles of irrigation pipe on the first golf-course site and the presence of over 1,000 workers laboring on the various projects of phase 1 marked additional milestones.[33]

Subsequently, on April 1, 1974, 180 employees of Mitchell Development Corporation of the Southwest moved into the first completed office building in Office Park. The building was a 50,000-square-foot cluster of four two-story modules surrounding an enclosed central courtyard covered with skylights. Like all other components of The Woodlands, it endeavored in both exterior and interior design to enhance the wooded environment. April, 1974, was, in fact, a banner month for The Woodlands. Construction in progress included a $1.5 million Information Center overlooking a 17-acre lake; the first neighborhood center, Sawmill Community Center, on a 25-acre tract, and planned eventually to contain a health-care center, an elementary school, a neighborhood park, and a day-care center; a townhouse cluster and a fifty-unit apartment complex; two industrial buildings in the Trade Center; and Grogan's Mill Village Square, including a professional office building, an enclosed shopping mall (The Wharf), and an indoor ice-skating rink. The Information Center in particular drew effusive praise from James W. Rush, vice-president of marketing for Mitchell Development Corporation of the Southwest, who described the two-cluster, geometrically connected forms surrounding a central land-

33. *Conroe Daily Courier,* January 24, March 10, 1974; *Houston Chronicle,* January 27, March 17, February 20, 1974; *Woodlands Sun,* February 5, 1974; *Houston Post,* March 17, March 24, 1974.

George P. Mitchell at opening day ceremonies, October 19, 1974.

scaped core as the "largest, most comprehensive and architecturally distinctive new town information center ever to be built," conveying "the spirit, lifestyle and woodsy feeling of The Woodlands."[34]

Succeeding months witnessed rapid progress toward completion of phase 1, although some delay resulted late in the summer from picketing by union carpenters in a contract dispute with a subcontractor which spread to include the Community Development Construction Corporation, a Mitchell Energy and Development Corporation subsidiary and the major building contractor in The Woodlands. Nonetheless, by early August workers had completed a second 50,000-square-foot office building in the Office Park and a fifty-unit apartment com-

34. *Conroe Daily Courier,* April 1, 1974; *Woodlands Sun,* April 3, 1974; *Houston Post,* April 7, April 28, 1974; *Houston Chronicle,* April 19, April 21, April 28, 1974.

J. Leonard Ivins at opening day ceremonies, October 19, 1974.

plex on the shores of 17-acre Lake Harrison, and a veteran Houston-based custom home builder had begun construction of the first of twenty-one single-family residences his company planned to build in Grogan's Mill Village.[35]

The opening of The Woodlands was originally scheduled for March but was postponed to August as construction lagged and workers failed to complete the infrastructure until July. It was finally held October, 1974. The company spared no effort to make the three-weekend event a gala and impressive affair. Festivities commenced with a parade of antique cars from Houston to The Woodlands and continued with the presentation to county officials of specially designed flags for Mont-

35. *Conroe Daily Courier*, July 22, August 14, August 16, August 20, 1974; *Houston Chronicle*, August 11, 1974; *Houston Post*, August 18, 1974.

63

The Woodlands Information Center, 1974.

gomery County and The Woodlands and speeches by Mitchell and U.S. Congressman Charles Wilson. Other events included dedication of The Woodlands post office; ice-skating exhibitions; an arts-and-crafts display; screening of a "Flash Gordon" film serial accompanied by comments from its star, Buster Crabbe; an archery exhibition by national and international champions, including a performance by William Shatner, star of the television series "Star Trek"; an exhibition of the works of Norman Rockwell; and day-long music provided by mariachi, country-and-western, and Dixieland bands.

Visitors, estimated at over 22,000, also had an opportunity to inspect nineteen model homes, twelve townhouses, fifty apartments, an intermediate school, The Woodlands Country Club, a health and racquet club, three office buildings, and the CCLC, including The Woodlands Inn and The Wharf (an 80,000-square-foot enclosed shopping mall on Lake Harrison).[36]

As 1974 drew to a close, The Woodlands, as its opening celebration indicated, appeared to be "a financially viable development" which offered a "stunning" amenities package to potential buyers.[37] Beneath the exterior glitter, however, major defects existed. Those deficiencies, exacerbated by a national recession, continuing neglect and parsimony of an uninterested Nixon administration, and extended controversy with HUD, were to drive Mitchell and his company to the brink of insolvency.

36. "Woodlands Village Chronicle," August 16, 1972; *Woodlands Newsletter,* October, 1974, pp. 1–3; November, 1974, pp. 1–2.

37. Booz-Allen, *New Communities,* H-V-1.

5. A New Town's Infancy

THE STRUGGLE FOR SURVIVAL, 1973–1974

The glamorous opening of The Woodlands in October, 1974, masked but did not negate a complex of deep-rooted problems. Those difficulties, both internal and external, kept Mitchell's new town in a precarious state for the next several years and severely taxed both his organizational skills and his companies' financial resources.

Not all the early difficulties experienced by The Woodlands resulted from internal deficiencies or managerial errors in judgment. By the end of 1972 fifteen new towns had been approved by HUD; by the same date strong and persistent signals indicated serious problems in the program.[1] First, the Nixon administration, never supportive of the new-town concept, became increasingly uninterested and in January, 1973, in reaction to inflation and economic recession, declared a moratorium on federal grants. A few months later the U.S. Office of Management and Budget (OMB) impounded a $7.5 million appropriation approved by Congress in August, 1972, for supplementary grants to new-town developers. Nixon's and OMB's actions shut off expected and urgently needed revenues for infrastructure building and forced all the new-

---

1. U.S. Congress, House, *Oversight Hearings on HUD New Communities Program: Hearings before a Subcommittee on Housing of the Committee on Banking and Currency,* 93rd Cong., 1st sess. (1973), pp. 1, 38. The fifteen new towns were Jonathan, Minn., St. Charles, Md., Park Forest South, Ill., Flower Mound, Tex.; Maumelle, Ark.; Cedar-Riverside, Minn.; Riverton, N.Y.; San Antonio Ranch, Tex.; Ganada, N.Y.; Soul City, N.C.; Harbison, S.C.; Lysander, N.Y.; Welfare Island, N.Y.; Shenandoah, Ga.; and The Woodlands, Tex.

community developers to fall back on their own resources.[2] Second, HUD lacked the organizational structure, expertise, and staff to administer the new community program efficiently or even adequately. George Romney, secretary of HUD from 1969 to 1972, an unquestioned friend of urban reform, ordered a reorganization of HUD which though well meaning had the effect of blurring lines of authority and program responsibility. The resultant infighting and low morale added to high staff turnovers, and administrative chaos at times rendered HUD literally nonfunctional. Also, try as he might, Romney never succeeded in gaining the president's ear. Orders issued in early 1972 for cuts in personnel hit HUD particularly hard.[3]

William Nicoson, first director of HUD's Office of New Community Development (ONCD) and a staunch supporter of the new-town concept who later resigned in protest over the lack of support for the program by the Nixon administration, had built up his staff from ten to thirty-five with authorization from Romney for a total of fifty when the order came down for a 20 percent cut.[4] The result, Nicoson later testified, was the loss of the department's best and most able personnel, a further lowering of morale, and, most important, an inability to administer the new-town program. Nicoson found the administration's policy penny-wise and pound-foolish in view of the fee payments to HUD required of the developers. A single $50 million twenty-year debenture guarantee which netted HUD $10 million in fees, in comparison to a "few extra dollars for salaries" for staff, struck Nicoson as "a good business investment."[5] He pointed to three problems, all stemming from failure to implement the funding envisioned by the 1970 legislation, which plagued the new-town developers and threatened to destroy the credibility of the program: inadequate staffing within HUD; heavy initial developer costs for infrastructure and the Nixon administration's failure to fund public service grants for that purpose; and the financial risk to developers entailed by innovative planning

2. Ibid., p. 5; Mildred F. Schmertz, "New Hopes, New Options, but No Money: Whatever Happened to Title VII?" *Architectural Record* 154 (December, 1973): 87. Schmertz predicted: "If the high public purpose embodied in the Federally Assisted New Communities program is destroyed through the indifference and apathy of the present administration, the new towns now under way will fall far short of their social and environmental goals. At best, most of them will become upper-middle and upper-income enclaves. At worst some of them will be abandoned."

3. M. Carter McFarland, *Federal Government and Urban Problem: HUD—Successes, Failures, and the Fate of Our Cities,* pp. 42–45.

4. U.S. Congress, House, *Oversight Hearings,* pp. 8, 28. By spring, 1973, HUD's staff had risen to forty-four, five of whom were professional planners. Ibid., pp. 132–33.

5. Ibid., p. 17.

and impoundment by OMB of the congressional appropriation intended to help developers defray those costs. For these reasons, Nicoson stated, the 1970 legislation had not realized its potential. "Yet," he concluded, "I am nevertheless hopeful that the future will see a reassessment and rededication of support on the part of the administration."[6]

Unfortunately, the Nixon administration's interest did not increase, nor did leadership of HUD improve after Romney's departure. His successor, James Lynn (1972–75), not only lacked professional expertise but also made little effort to bring order out of chaos other than to appoint a general manager directly responsible for the new-community program. In fact, Lynn may have taken over HUD with instructions "to maintain its dormancy and beyond that, to reduce further whatever else could be reduced."[7] Carla Hills, secretary of HUD from 1975 to 1977, though intelligent and industrious, likewise possessed neither professional experience nor an inclination to strive for badly needed reorganization. Like her predecessor, Hills dedicated her efforts more to reducing operating costs than to supporting HUD's programs.[8]

The disordered state of affairs in HUD and the administration's failure to support the new-communities program received ample, and at times colorful, criticism during congressional hearings in the spring of 1973. Lewis Manilow, speaking for a group of delegates representing the League of New Community Developers, complained that the Nixon administration and HUD had given the program "only very modest support" and had failed to make available most of the loans and grants provided for by the 1970 legislation. "We want," he said, "to build communities which have a balanced socioeconomic population, not upper middle-class suburbs. We want to fulfill our commitments to innovation, citizen participation, ecological enhancement, and social programming and still retain financial feasibility. To do this, loan guarantees alone are insufficient. We need two supports from the administration—(1) effective and prompt administration, and (2) supplementary assistance."

Manilow applauded the dedication of a dwindling group of HUD staff members who had helped fifteen new communities survive the HUD "labyrinth" but pointed also to the "discouraging . . . fact that the review and monitoring process is getting more complex, more demanding, more tedious, and hence much more expensive. . . . As of this moment, the program marks time without strong leadership and direc-

6. Ibid., pp. 4–5.
7. McFarland, *Federal Government and Urban Problems,* pp. 45–46.
8. Ibid., pp. 46–47.

tion."[9] In the same vein Mark Freeman, the executive director of the League of New Community Developers, cited a study by Decisions Sciences Corporation which showed an average thirty-eight-month time span from submission of preapplication to final HUD approval. Freeman added: "As presently administered the program works an undue hardship. . . . The process is too long, too costly, and too cumbersome in its administration. It has caused developers to commit approximately $1 million exclusive of land costs per project, and 3 years of time in order to obtain assistance. . . . The problem does not stop here. Even after finally negotiating a project agreement, developers are faced with unconscionable delays in drawing down funds and in securing consent for proposed changes."[10]

Donald L. Huber, developer of Newfields, a new town outside Dayton, Ohio, and a member of the Board of Directors of the League of New Community Developers, bitterly denounced HUD's insistence on demonstrated developer commitment to the social goals of the 1970 legislation despite its failure to provide promised subsidies. HUD, Huber complained, demanded that new-town developers provide low- and moderate-income housing; establish a comprehensive program of social, educational, and health services; and be innovative, and yet refused, either willfully or otherwise, to "make a similar commitment to the developers to deliver the requisite housing subsidies at the time the developer schedules them to be built. . . . If the housing subsidy cannot be made available when the developer is ready to phase them in his construction program, the resulting delay usually means a substantial increase in holding costs which can only be passed on later to builders in the form of higher land costs."[11]

In more flamboyant style Carlos Campbell, an urban planner and former special assistant to the assistant secretary for community planning and management in HUD, excoriated mindless urban growth which encouraged polarization of racial and income groups, discharged millions of tons of pollutants into the skies, and erected monolithic megastructures and other "antihuman" artifacts. He asserted: "In the midst of all of this chaos and confusion, and while . . . armed with a powerful and comprehensive legislative mandate, . . . the executive branch, in general, and the Department of Housing and Urban Development, in particular, has seemingly taken the position of 'letting the lions and the Christians go at it.'"[12]

9. U.S. Congress, House, *Oversight Hearings,* p. 36.
10. Ibid., p. 46.
11. Ibid., p. 73.
12. Ibid., p. 213.

When William Nicoson resigned as director of the Office of New Community Development, Campbell recalled, "things came to a screeching halt," morale plummeted, and a number of key personnel chose to resign. Campbell also questioned the capacity of the existing HUD staff to perform its responsibilities and indicted an organizational structure which bred "confusion as to what responsibility and authority exist between the Secretary of HUD, the General Manager of the Community Development Corporation, the Assistant Secretary for Community Planning and Management, the Director of the Office of New Community Planning, and the various division directors within the Office of New Community Development."[13]

The subsequent financial failures experienced by most of the new towns verified these charges and revealed additional faults. Beginning in December, 1974, with the near bankruptcy of Riverton, a new community outside Rochester, New York, and HUD's assumption in March, 1975, of a $1 million interest payment for the financially pressed developers of Park Forest South, Illinois, the new towns reached crisis points in their financial affairs.[14] By midsummer, 1976, of the twelve projects holding federally guaranteed debentures, all but The Woodlands reported total or near bankruptcy—insolvencies which forced HUD to assume their interest payments or to arrange for refinancing in a futile attempt to salvage something from the debacle.[15]

While developers typically singled out HUD, the Nixon administration, and OMB as the sources of their plight, other factors bore equal if not greater responsibility. Those factors included unrealistic cash-flow projections, the economic recession and an end to the boom in home sales, developers' insufficient financial resources, mismanagement by

13. Ibid., p. 215.
14. Helene V. Smookler, "Administration Hara-Kiri: Implementation of the Urban Growth and New Community Development Act," *Annals of the American Academy of Political and Social Science* 422 (November, 1975): 137–38; Scott Jacobs, "New Towns—or Ghost Towns?" *Planning* 41 (January, 1975): 15–18. Flower Mound, Tex., and Cedar-Riverside, Minn., had exhausted development funds of $18 million and $24 million, respectively, by January, 1975. Jonathan, Minn., after making a successful beginning and reaching a population of 2,250, halted further development and began seeking a buyer during late 1974. *Washington Post,* January 15, 1975. See also "Can 'New Towns' Survive the Economic Crunch?" *Business Week* 2367 (February 10, 1975): 43–44.
15. Richard Karp, "Building Chaos: The New Town Program Is a Multimillion-Dollar Mess," *Barron's National Business and Financial Weekly* 56 (September 6, 1976): 3, 8, 10, 12. By summer, 1976, HUD had committed $280 million in debenture guarantees. By that time five projects reported severe financial straits, and six acknowledged bankruptcy. See also "New Towns That Haunt HUD," *Business Week* 2427 (April 12, 1976): 36; "Picking Up the Pieces of HUD's New Towns," *Business Week* 2446 (August 23, 1976): 30.

developers and their staffs, poor locations of projects in terms of their potential to attract residents and industry, and opposition from political and environmental groups. Ganada, New York, is often cited as the program's major failure and the most seriously mismanaged project. The developers of Ganada, originally planned as a 9,000-acre, 50,000-population new town, poured about $32 million into the project between April, 1972, the date of HUD's $22 million debenture guarantee, and late 1974, when HUD took over the development corporation's loan interest payments. At that point construction consisted of a school, a man-made lake, one black-topped road, and two model homes, one of which burned to the ground. The developer's additional debts included $11 million in land-purchase mortgages, $3 million owed to various creditors, and $800,000 in unpaid real estate taxes. Significantly, of the $32 million charged to development, only $12.8 million actually went into construction, while nearly $20 million went for salaries, consultants' fees, interest payments, and miscellaneous administrative costs.[16]

Newfields, Ohio, suffered a similar lag in development despite an expenditure of $18 million over a thirty-month period. By that time total construction in the project consisted of thirty-seven homes, an Olympic-size swimming pool, a nine-acre lake, and a community center. In October, 1976, HUD belatedly announced that its investigation showed Newfields to be "financially and economically infeasible as a full-scale Title VII new community."[17]

Two other new towns, Soul City, North Carolina, and San Antonio Ranch, Texas, underwent somewhat different but equally nonproductive experiences. Soul City possessed unique features as a planned free-standing community, sponsorship by a black entrepreneur, and a location in an economically depressed area. After nearly six years of planning and development, plus some $5 million in federal grants and debenture guarantees, the project consisted of one empty industrial building and a number of mobile homes occupied by the developer and staff members. While the developer blamed HUD and a growing social conservatism during the early 1970s for the lack of progress, a nearby metropolitan newspaper charged the developer with misman agement and even political opportunism.[18] San Antonio Ranch like-

16. Karp, "Building Chaos," pp. 3, 8, 10, 12; "New Towns That Haunt HUD," p. 36.
17. Martin Mayer, The Builders: Houses, People, Neighborhoods, Government, Money, p. 92.
18. Washington Post, January 15, 1975; Ed McCahill, "Soul City—More Than a Pea Patch," Planning 41 (August, 1975): 20–21. Among other charges the newspaper alleged that the developer, Floyd McKissick, had become a Republican in 1972 in expectation

wise failed to move much beyond the drawing board, but for quite different, if not more easily discernible, reasons. The project developers began poorly by shrouding their plans in secrecy before making preapplication with HUD. Consequently, interested members of local government entities, when finally apprised of the project, expressed outrage and opposition. Furthermore, the developers, with HUD's apparent acquiescence and in technical violation of the law, chose to prepare the Environmental Impact Statement themselves. In the process they obscured—according to local environmentalists—the effect of the proposed project on the Edwards Aquifer, San Antonio's primary water-supply source. To compound their problems further, the developers, or one of their number, tried at times to coerce opponents into changing their minds, a tactic which resulted in an even greater resolve to defeat the project. In the end the combination of secretiveness, insensitivity to legitimate concerns expressed by local politicians (particularly over the project's possible diversion of federal funds from the city), and the failure to submit a nonpartisan environmental impact statement led to solidification of political opposition, a time-consuming court trial, and the demise of San Antonio Ranch as a viable new-town project.[19]

By 1981, HUD had foreclosed on nine of the new towns. Three of the remaining four communities—St. Charles, Maryland; Maumelle, Arkansas, and Harbison, South Carolina—suffered severe financial straits but escaped foreclosure because HUD deemed them "socially and environmentally viable." HUD rescued them through refinancing, agreeing to partial repayments, and accepting promises of future reimbursements.[20]

---

of receiving $14 million from the Nixon administration, the amount of HUD's debenture guarantee. Some of Soul City's problems stemmed from the fact that the developer held title to only one-third of the project's proposed 5,180-acre site and had options on the remainder. The financial agreement with HUD made purchase of the additional land nearly impossible because full federal funding depended on the developer's attracting enough industry to provide three hundred jobs.

19. The foregoing summary is from Wayt T. and Roberta Watterson, *The Politics of New Communities: A Case Study of San Antonio Ranch.* The Wattersons conclude that San Antonio Ranch "represented the worst in political maneuvering and conspiratorial conduct at various levels of government, was the first Title VII new community whose legal right to be developed was tested and upheld, and was, more than any other single cause, responsible for the changes in HUD's requirements and its attitudes toward its role as public trustee." Ibid., p. 118.

20. Mary-Margaret Wantuck, "Those New Towns, 15 Years Later," *Nation's Business* 71 (October, 1983): 42–43. One investigator states that by summer, 1975, HUD's Office of Policy Development and Research favored abandoning the new-community program for an emphasis on planned unit developments (PUDs). McCahill, "Soul City," p. 21. HUD

Although The Woodlands avoided the deepest afflictions experienced by other new towns, the project followed an equally tortuous path. The same delays, fiscal omissions, and overall administrative chaos cited by other new-town developers and former HUD officials also plagued The Woodlands during its critical start-up period. A total of twenty-seven months elapsed from the time HUD reviewed the pre-application to the final closing of the Project Agreement. Another twelve-month delay, which prevented closing of land sales, occurred from January, 1973, to January, 1974, because of conflict with the Federal Housing Administration over the legal status of The Woodlands Community Association; the same debate contributed to a long delay in approval of the project for mortgage guarantees by the Veterans Administration. Equally frustrating and sometimes costly time delays resulted from the three-to-six-month HUD reviews of routine requests for changes in the development plan.[21]

In addition to HUD's structural, leadership, and personnel deficiencies, an adversary relationship that early arose between the federal agency and the developers further limited administrative efficiency.[22] By March, 1972, for example, Mitchell's staff had become convinced that HUD viewed them as "rich, arrogant Texans." Their equally uninformed view of HUD personnel as incompetent, petty bureaucrats so impeded relations that direct negotiations for approval of the project were turned over to Piper and Marbury, a Baltimore law firm.[23] These distorted perspectives not only undermined working relations but also contributed to HUD's unsound judgment in February, 1973, that the financial viability of The Woodlands did not depend on grant

terminated the new-community program on September 30, 1983, after expending $590 million in loan guarantees and grants. The overall failure of the program led one former general manager of HUD's defunct NCDC to observe, "I think we've demonstrated that the government doesn't belong in this business, and I hope we have learned that and don't try it again." Wantuck, "Those New Towns," p. 42.

21. Booz-Allen, New Communities, H-VII-1–H-VII-12.

22. U.S. Congress, House, Oversight Hearings, p. 130. A HUD deputy assistant secretary for community planning and management argued that HUD's slow review of applications stemmed from its concern for the environment and economic feasibility, local community problems, and faulty interagency coordination. Representative Ashley rebutted that argument with the observation: "That doesn't really begin to reflect at all what we have heard from the developers. . . . They have really talked about some very severe staffing problems within ONCD, and they have talked about lack of any kind of morale. They even talk about . . . a sort of antideveloper bias, adversary proceedings, rather than a cooperative undertaking. And some are talking about the possibility of bringing lawsuits in order to cause ONCD, FHA, and HUD to live up to their agreements."

23. "The Woodlands Chronicle," p. 50.

assistance. This determination remained a bone of contention which aggravated relations and kept grant support for The Woodlands virtually nonexistent through 1974.[24]

The failure of HUD and other federal agencies to deliver supplementary grants affected The Woodlands more adversely than did administrative inefficiency. Like other new-town developers, Mitchell and his staff fully expected grants to be immediately forthcoming and based much of their planning on that expectation. Up to 1975, however, The Woodlands had received only one grant—$75,000 from the Department of Health, Education, and Welfare for a library.[25]

As early as February, 1973, some members of Mitchell's group, either prescient or simply pessimistic because of previous negotiations with HUD, expressed their belief that federal funds would not be available during the first critical years of construction. Their pessimism prompted Len Ivins to warn Mitchell of the possibility and to suggest the need to plan an alternative course. He wrote Mitchell: "Obviously, nobody likes to eliminate projects and programs that are so important to people and the environment, but our other commitments will compel us to cut back in The Woodlands if we do not get the promised federal assistance and we had better establish our priorities now both for our benefit and so that we can advise HUD of our decision."[26] Despite such forebodings, phase 1 development proceeded as planned. By spring, 1974, however, the lack of revenues and heavy-construction expenditures made it impossible to continue to acquiesce in the nondelivery of the expected grants. On May 20, Mitchell wrote to Senator Tower enclosing a letter of the same date to Secretary Lynn protesting HUD's policy. "HUD," Mitchell informed Tower, "has been grossly unfair to our project. . . . Many ancillary grants were scheduled and although we have made numerous appeals, we have received no new grants." He continued that, to his dismay and that of his associates, "in the last two months, we discovered that various grants were given to other projects, but for some reason we were being discriminated against. We have asked the Secretary to meet with us, to make amends, and to let us participate in order for us to meet our social obligations. . . . The failure to receive such grants would affect us considerably and would eliminate the availability of housing in the low and medium range groups."

24. Booz-Allen, New Communities, H-III-9, H-III-10, H-IV-21.

25. Ibid., H-VII-6. Mitchell claimed that grants for sewer, water, and drainage systems were "assumed" in the project's financial plan and stated that he would not have committed Mitchell Energy and Development Corporation to the project if he had not expected to receive federal funds. Ibid., H-III-10.

26. J. Leonard Ivins to George P. Mitchell, February 20, 1973, WDC Papers.

His group, Mitchell assured Tower, remained committed to its "purpose to develop this project for all the people of Houston, not just the upper class. It is with this concept that we join[ed] with the government in trying to carry out this project."[27]

The failure of HUD to meet its obligations produced in-house discussion about instituting legal action on the basis of discrimination and denial of substantive due process, which constituted a breach of the Project Agreement. Mitchell's legal counsel estimated that HUD had reserved or approved supplementary grants for twelve new towns totaling $22,837,194, plus $73,790,082 in basic grant support. Although the agreed-to Financial Plan included grants to The Woodlands during the development period of $33,628,798, in the first year none of the grants had been received.

These failures plus inflated development costs and increased expenditures to counter the scarcity of mortgage financing and energy shortages, meant that the peak cash requirement for the project had risen from an original $61,956,000 to $98,680,000. Thus, to meet its financial and development obligations provided for in the Project Agreement, The Woodlands needed an additional $36 million.

Mitchell's attorney suggested short-term, long-term, and interim remedies for The Woodlands' grave financial condition and HUD's failures. The proposed short-term solution provided that HUD should immediately make available a grant of $2,162,806 for planning assistance and an interest-free loan of $20 million plus the previously agreed-on funds for water and sewer facilities. Finally, HUD should provide all other grants to ensure equal and nondiscriminatory treatment of The Woodlands. As a long-term—and highly unlikely—remedy HUD should make every effort to bring about congressional amendment of the 1970 legislation to increase the allowable debenture guarantee for a single project to $100 million and should approve an additional $50 million issue by The Woodlands. The interim solution provided that HUD would immediately approve the release from lien of security of some 1,000 acres in the Metro Center, which The Woodlands could then use as security to obtain a $15 million loan from private sources.[28] Of the remedies suggested, only the interim remedy subsequently received full HUD approval, and it followed a tortuous path to completion.

The national economic decline beginning in 1972 and the Arab oil embargo in 1973 were additional, and even less controllable, external factors responsible for The Woodlands' early financial difficulties.

27. George P. Mitchell to Sen. John G. Tower, May 20, 1974, WDC Papers.
28. "The Woodlands-Grants," memorandum, June 25, 1974, WDC Papers.

At the time of The Woodlands' preapplication the nation and the Houston area were enjoying a boom economy. Yet despite market forecasts which exuded rosy optimism for the future, signs of trouble existed in upward spiraling interest rates, increasingly tight investment money, and soaring construction costs. Nonetheless, in the Houston area peak housing construction occurred during 1970–71, and the top sales period followed in 1971–72. Housing starts began to decline in 1972 and decreased each year thereafter, just as The Woodlands began construction. At the same time, increasing scarcity of mortgage financing bottomed out during 1974 and an accompanying rise in interest rates to 8.7 percent forced The Woodlands Development Corporation to help finance builders in The Woodlands. To add to already burdensome financial woes, inflationary costs of labor and materials significantly increased development expenses and forced an ultimate rise in housing prices.[29]

In the midst of a faltering economy and the near collapse of the real estate market, the Arab oil embargo of 1973 and the resultant gasoline shortage further added to the troubles afflicting The Woodlands. Frightened by rises in gasoline prices and the threat of future gasoline shortages, prospective buyers and renters of homes in the new town began to look nearer Houston and to opt for housing in one of a number of available single- and multifamily developments nearer the metropolitan core.[30]

It is apparent that the economic decline, executive branch parsimony and neglect, and ineffective administration by HUD had a serious impact on the financial viability of The Woodlands, as they did on all the other Title VII new towns. It is equally true that internal organizational deficiencies, unrealistic expectations, and unwise managerial decisions contributed as much if not more to the financial weaknesses of The Woodlands.

Internal organizational defects in The Woodlands Development Corporation included an excessively large staff of 365 persons. The overstaffing resulted in extremely high operating expenses at a time when austerity rather than extravagance should have been the rule. Also, the organizational structure of The Woodlands Development Corporation did not lend itself to productive management or effective cost control. In the corporation's original chain of command the chief financial officer and the general manager of the corporation functioned apart from one another and from other components of the organiza-

29. Booz-Allen, *New Communities,* H-VI-1–H-VI-10.
30. Ibid., H-VI-1, H-VI-3.

tion.[31] Consequently, one office often did not know what the other was doing. Thus the general manager of The Woodlands Development Corporation apologized to HUD in July, 1973, for failure to obtain HUD's prior approval for the transfer of land to an "interested person"– an omission which could be judged a default under the Project Agreement—with the explanation that the oversight resulted from defects in existing corporate procedures. Thereafter, he assured HUD, under newly instituted policy, a specific written opinion from corporate lawyers that all HUD approvals had been obtained would be required before transfer documents were presented to a company officer.[32]

A year later, however, another member of the Mitchell group complained to a colleague that a contract proposal which he had submitted to the company's legal department for review had been misrouted and buried on the desk of a company officer for three weeks. "It is my opinion," he wrote, "that this is an example of a bureaucracy which is not functional, and one must wonder how anything is accomplished."[33]

These organizational weaknesses, once apparent, could be relatively easily remedied. Errors in managerial judgment, however, by their very nature did not lend themselves to quick or easy reversal. The decision to invest heavily in non–Title VII development during phase 1 construction lacked financial prudence and at the same time labeled The Woodlands a prestige community intended for the middle and upper classes. Each of these errors had major repercussions.

While some HUD officials found phase 1 construction activity impressive and of high quality, others suspected a lack of commitment to the original social objectives of the program. Hence very early in the development process HUD began pressing Mitchell and his staff for assurances of policies designed to attract minorities, low- and moderate-income families, and the elderly to The Woodlands. In July, 1972, Samuel E. Jackson, assistant secretary for community planning and management in HUD, informed Mitchell: "I continue to be concerned that you at the earliest possible time demonstrate your commitment to the Affirmative Action goals of the Title VII program. This includes hiring of professional staff, involvement in planning at the earliest stages . . . , and communications with real estate brokers and other firms to make minority group members aware of business opportunities to be made available in the new community."[34] Jackson's fears would undoubtedly have been greater if he had known that the cor-

31. Ibid., H-VIII-1, H-VIII-3, H-VIII-9.
32. Robert W. McGee to Edward M. Lamont, July 24, 1973, WDC Papers.
33. James Blackburn to James Veltman, July 15, 1974, WDC Papers.
34. Samuel C. Jackson to George P. Mitchell, July 25, 1972, WDC Papers.

poration favored a cautious policy in regard to advertising business opportunities in the new town in minority publications during early stages of development because of existing market restraints and the desire to avoid promising more than could be delivered.[35] The concern of HUD officials about corporate commitment to programs designed to attract minority, low- and moderate-income groups, and the elderly dominated a meeting with Mitchell's staff in May, 1973. The persistent emphasis on those topics by HUD representatives during the session led one member of The Woodlands group to observe afterward, "It is becoming increasingly obvious to me that unless we confront the issue [in house] . . . we may reinforce already blooming negative attitudes concerning our project."[36] Once planted, and regardless of truth, the suspicion of a lack of commitment to social goals spread, intensifying the adversary relationship with HUD. Not the least of the results was a heightened and continuing tendency of HUD officials to question unduly some legitimate financial transactions and requests for program changes.

The lack of financial prudence inherent in the decision to spend large sums on prestige-type development during the first stage of construction quickly became apparent. As noted earlier, by midsummer, 1974, soaring construction expenditures, inordinately high administrative expenses, and the failure of expected federal grants to materialize had placed The Woodlands Development Corporation and the Mitchell company in a state of severe financial stress.[37] By then Mitchell Energy and Development Corporation had a capital investment of $28 million in improvements at The Woodlands—an outlay which caused some oil-and-gas-oriented members of the parent company's board of

35. Larry Thomas to David Hendricks, May 26, 1972, WDC Papers. Thomas cited this corporate preference in regard to the wisdom of giving a story to *Black Enterprise* about opportunities for minorities in The Woodlands. He also stated: "Running a story in *Black Enterprise* about minority opportunities . . . in and of itself will cause us no problems. In fact, it may be to our advantage to do so; one advantage is that it will help us define quite early the limits of minority involvement in the first phase of development and will help us test the validity of those limits. Another advantage is that it forces us to deal with the thorny question of the implications of HUD money on the attitudes of minorities."

36. Larry Thomas to Charles Kelly, May 30, 1973, WDC Papers. A HUD official informed the general manager of WDC on May 17, 1973, "While I am generally impressed with The Woodlands' overall implementation strategy, I want to see more positive efforts made to provide for low and moderate income housing at a pace comparable to that noted in the Development Plan." William Sorrentino to Robert McGee, May 17, 1973, WDC Papers.

37. Interview with Robinson G. Lapp, February 23, 1981; interview with Paul Wommack, November 1, 1982.

directors to protest. Some of the more disenchanted began to rail against the "Columbia mafia" on the real estate side whose financial excesses had driven the company into a quagmire of debt from which it might not escape.[38]

To extricate his company from the edge of financial disaster, Mitchell launched a campaign in July, 1974, to obtain HUD's approval of interim and short-term remedies. On July 29 he asked HUD to allow The Woodlands Development Corporation to borrow $15 million, using land in the Metro Center as security. HUD responded with a promise to review the request as "expeditiously as possible" and in the meantime authorized the corporation to proceed with tentative arrangements to borrow up to $5 million.[39] At a subsequent meeting with HUD in mid-August, Mitchell admitted that construction on the project was lagging approximately five months behind schedule because of heavy rains during the previous spring. He also pointed out, however, that all of the land programmed for first-year construction had been placed under contract or deed and that twelve home builders were at work in The Woodlands. On August 22, after HUD raised the specter of filing a charge of default by The Woodlands Development Corporation for failure to maintain required net current assets, HUD approved the borrowing of $5 million but postponed authorization of the remaining $10 million pending further investigation. In late August, 1974, The Woodlands Development Corporation obtained $2 million from Chase Manhattan Bank and in October borrowed $3 million from the Provident National Bank of Philadelphia.[40]

In its usual desultory fashion HUD delayed authorizing the borrowing of the remaining $10 million until December 20, 1974. HUD also attached a number of conditions to its authorization, most of which dealt with the elimination of projected peak debts. Specifically, HUD stipulated that Mitchell Development Corporation of the Southwest and

38. "The Woodlands—Grants," memorandum, June 25, 1974; interview with Charles Kelly, August 31, 1982; interview with Paul Wommack, November 1, 1982. An investigation conducted during 1978 conclulded that while organizational structure "was not the only cause of the poor operating and financial results, the parent company considered itself to have been 'burned' by the degree of autonomy it had generated, and reacted strongly in the other direction." Kenneth Leventhal and Company, *Report on Intensive Studies of Selected New Community Projects*, p. 11; hereafter cited as Leventhal and Company, *Intensive Studies*.

39. John Martin Jones, Jr., to Albert F. Trevino, July 29, 1974, WDC Papers. Jones, a member of the law firm Piper and Marbury, confirmed the request by Mitchell in a telephone conversation with HUD on that day.

40. Booz-Allen, *New Communities*, H-III-11; Otto G. Stolz to J. Leonard Ivins, December 20, 1974, WDC Papers.

Mitchell Energy and Development Corporation must guarantee elimination by 1978 of a predicted Woodlands Development Corporation cash deficit of $26,744,000 by contributing $5.4 million of equity to The Woodlands Development Corporation. Of that sum, $2.6 million was to be paid by February 1, 1975, and the remaining $2.8 million was to be paid on a month-to-month basis as needed by The Woodlands Development Corporation. HUD also promised to use its best efforts to help The Woodlands in its efforts to obtain federal grants.[41]

Receipt of the $15 million in loans enabled Mitchell and The Woodlands to weather the financial crisis. It did not, of course, heal the causes which had led to near catastrophe. Mitchell, who had not previously engaged in day-to-day management of the project, now began to play a more active role, particularly in managerial reorganization, reductions in personnel, and scaled-down development activity.

41. Booz-Allen, *New Communities,* H-III-12; Stolz to Ivins, December 20, 1974, WDC Papers. HUD also required that the Woodlands Development Corporation must obtain the loan at the best available interest and repayment terms, that Mitchell Development Corporation of the Southwest must guarantee repayment, that the loan must be secured by a lien on land in the Metro Center, and that proceeds of the loan must be used for actual costs of land acquisition or development and for repayment of the loans from Chase Manhattan Bank and Provident National Bank.

6. A New Town in Crisis

The Woodlands Development Corporation's financial crisis, commencing in August, 1974, and only temporarily abating in December, led to a number of organizational changes designed to streamline staff and centralize authority. A concurrent shift away from social planning to a greater emphasis on sales and marketing also stemmed directly from financial stringencies. Unfortunately, this change buttressed the scoffers and doubters in their belief that new towns in general and The Woodlands in particular paid only lip service to the social goals of the 1970 legislation while profit remained the paramount, if not the exclusive, aim.[1]

George Mitchell's assumption of more direct control of The Woodlands Development Corporation constituted the most significant structural modification and forecast the departure of Len Ivins. Reactions to Ivins within the company remain mixed to this day. Those close to him and others less appreciative of his talents agree that the present physical character of The Woodlands indelibly carries his stamp and is a tribute to his leadership.[2] It is also true that some officers of the parent company, appalled by the deepening debt generated by the real estate division, felt that they had been "burned" by the autonomy enjoyed by Ivins and reacted strongly in the other direction.[3] By mid-January, 1975, and the emergence of an even greater crisis in the af-

1. Booz-Allen, *New Communities,* H-II-4.
2. Interview with Charles Kelly, August 31, 1982; interview with Paul Wommack, November 1, 1982.
3. Leventhal and Company, *Intensive Studies,* p. 11. Leventhal's investigation dis-

fairs of The Woodlands Development Corporation, Ivins's departure became certain. From that time some of the original members of Mitchell's planning and development staff and most of the corporate officers imported from Columbia, Maryland, either resigned or fell victim to the reorganizational ax. James Veltman, who chafed against reductions in his responsibilities, was among the first of the former, while the latter group included original mainstays like Robert Hartsfield and latecomers like Sam Calleri, vice-president of finance.[4]

The reorganized command structured of The Woodlands Development Corporation, inaugurated in January, 1975, was designed to coordinate more closely the activities of various departments by funneling budget and operating projections through a four-man management committee to the president and from him to George Mitchell. The unwieldy and costly staff was reduced from 365 to 160. The entire Department of Institutional Development, directed by Charles Kelly, was eliminated.[5]

The abandonment of so-called software programs signaled by elimination of the department responsible for social planning and Kelly's subsequent departure reflected Len Ivins's public statement before his own departure that The Woodlands Development Corporation would combat its financial crisis through "a holding action with minimum staff, minimum overhead, whatever is required to get through the next year and possibly 1976."[6] The virtual scuttling of social planning provided more ammunition to critics of the new town, who undoubtedly found self-justification in the prediction of two urban planners that "most of the new towns completed 25 years hence will not fail; they will succeed, in a moderate and dull way. They will yield a small profit, provide a modicum of low- and middle-income housing, manage to stick fairly close to the original development plans . . . and present no particular threat to the environment." The residents' style of living, the two experts asserted, would not be "too different from that of other suburban dwellers. More persons may live comfortably, walk to work, have easier access to assorted recreational facilities, and perhaps even feel a

closed that the revamped organizational structure included "tight reporting and approval control at the parent level, on finance, budgeting, accounting, and legal functions. Significantly, hiring of all management personnel must be handled through the parent personnel group, and the 'number-two' executive at the parent company personally reviews all such requests before hiring is approved."

4. James Veltman to J. Leonard Ivins, October 3, 1974, WDC Papers; Booz-Allen, New Communities, H-III-13; interview with Robinson G. Lapp, February 23, 1981.
5. Booz-Allen, New Communities, H-III-3, H-VII-2.
6. Quoted in Washington Post, January 12, 1975.

greater sense of belonging. . . . What is far less certain is whether these few towns will serve the poor and disadvantaged, achieve a greater socio-economic mix, spur significant innovations or, even more important, serve broader ends."[7]

In fairness to Mitchell and other developers of new towns, most of whom experienced even more severe financial crises during late 1974 and early 1975, it is important to note again the economic realities which dictated fiscal austerity. By the end of 1974 residential dwellings constructed in The Woodlands totaled 62; this figure contrasted sharply with the development program projection of 1,450 for 1973 and another 825 units scheduled for 1974. Total office and retail space constructed amounted to 479,799 square feet with only 81 percent occupancy; industrial space totaled 100,000 square feet, all vacant.[8] These numbers, combined with high land-purchase and infrastructure costs, heavy overhead and carrying expenses, and lack of expected federal grants, meant that the budgetary ax had to be wielded somewhere, and nonincome-producing social planning seemed the logical place. As a friendly observer sagely commented early in the social-planning process at The Woodlands, "Mitchell is . . . sell[ing] land and houses, not a textbook about life in 2001," and in the last analysis the success or failure of The Woodlands hinged on his ability to accomplish the former, not the latter.[9] Otto G. Stolz, general manager of HUD's Office of New Community Development, echoed much of that sentiment in his reaction to undeniable reports in January, 1975, that the new-town program was in "economic and political disarray" and the announcement of a HUD moratorium on new-community applications. "The reality of new town development has set in," Stolz declared. "The blue sky thinking and the dreaming has ended and the reality has set in that this is just a damn difficult mode of development from a management standpoint."[10]

In the midst of Mitchell's efforts to economize and provide improved management for The Woodlands Development Corporation, HUD initiated a new crisis which diverted his attention from reorganization and also precipitated sweeping executive dismissals, including the removal of Len Ivins as president of The Woodlands Development Corporation and his replacement by Leland Carter in an acting capacity. On January 16, 1975, HUD served The Woodlands Development Corporation with a notice of default, charging the company with violation of sec-

7. Ibid.
8. Booz-Allen, *New Communities,* H-III-12.
9. "Woodlands Village Chronicle" (manuscript in WDC Papers), October 16–17, 1971.
10. Quoted in *Washington Post,* January 12, 1975.

tion 6.18 of the Project Agreement. That section required HUD's prior written consent for any transaction involving an "Interested Person," broadly defined as Mitchell, his family, Mitchell Energy and Development Corporation, Mitchell Development Corporation of the Southwest, and officers and directors of The Woodlands Development Corporation. The prohibitions also included 20 percent shareholders of Mitchell Energy and Development Corporation and Mitchell Development Corporation of the Southwest and all corporations, partnerships, and other business organizations in which The Woodlands Development Corporation, Mitchell Energy and Development Corporation, Mitchell Development Corporation of the Southwest, or a 20 percent shareholder in Mitchell Energy and Development Corporation owned or controlled 10 percent or more of interest. Specific violations included transactions involving rental of Woodlands Development Corporation office space, sharing or exchange of personnel, and ownership of The Woodlands Gas Company and the Stewart-Woodlands Title Company, Inc.[11]

Subsequent notices from HUD extended the default to include sections in the Project Agreement dealing with "Non-Reimbursable Items" and "Restricted Subsidiaries" which prohibited such subsidiaries from engaging in non–Title VII activities (land acquisition and development) and restricted borrowing and land transfers by both the development company and its affiliates.[12] The Woodlands Development Corporation had thirty days in which to "cure" the defaults or suffer further consequences, but on February 14, 1975, HUD extended the time limit to April 1, 1974.[13]

The most troublesome defaults involved those which violated the Project Agreement stipulation that funds obtained from the sale of the $50 million of federally guaranteed debentures could be expended only for costs of land acquisition and development. Thus HUD specifically cited $6,346,273 in transactions involving the Community Development and Construction Corporation, a subsidiary of Mitchell Energy and Development Corporation, for road, drainage, and water- and sewer-system construction plus various town and community projects. Other

11. Otto G. Stolz to J. Leonard Ivins, January 16, 1975, WDC Papers; R. N. Hinton to Edward Lee, November 28, 1977, WDC Papers.
12. Otto G. Stolz to Woodlands Development Corporation, n.d., WDC Papers. Stolz wrote five letters, in addition to the original letter of default, in response to a cure proposed by the corporation in a letter dated February 14, 1975. One letter is dated March 13, 1975, which makes it reasonable to conclude that the others were written between February 14 and March 13, 1975.
13. Otto G. Stolz to Woodlands Development Corporation, March 14, 1975, WDC Papers.

major violations claimed by HUD included $4,093,040.20 paid by The Woodlands Development Corporation to Mitchell Energy and Development Corporation as reimbursement for funds expended in its behalf for payroll and expenses; payment of $295,000 to Mitchell Development Corporation of the Southwest for the same purposes; payments to George Mitchell and Associates, the predecessor of Mitchell Development Corporation of the Southwest, of approximately $1,298,800 for the same reasons plus another $3,007,243 as reimbursement for Woodlands Development Corporation vouchers, overhead allocations, and purchase-money mortgages; payment to Mitchell Development Corporation of the Southwest of approximately $103,687 for land purchase and ad valorem taxes; $1,192.55 paid to Mitchell and Mitchell Corporation for land release plus $24,046.70 for reimbursement for payment of ad valorem taxes; payment of $13,175 to Design Index, Inc., for furniture and fixtures; $32,182 paid to Woodlands Nursery, Inc., for landscaping; and payment of $1,168,258 to Grogan's Mill Venture for pathways, a helipad, parking-area and tennis-facility expansion studies, resurfacing of roads and parking lots, road design and construction, landscaping, a boat dock and promenade, golf-course maintenance equipment, trash removal, and legal filing fees.[14]

While non-Title VII activity by subsidiaries constituted a major cause for the default notice, it is also conceivable that HUD's unexpected action resulted from its knowledge of the financial woes of The Woodlands and an understandable desire to protect the government's interest. Robinson G. Lapp, who joined The Woodlands Development Corporation in May, 1973, after service with the new town at Gananda, New York, and who took over relations with HUD in January, 1975, rejects "interested persons" violations as the true cause. "The real problem," Lapp believes, was that "we were running out of money . . . and that was reflected by a request in late 1974 that we be allowed to release an amount of land (in the Metro Center) in such a fashion that we could obtain some additional borrowing on that piece of land. . . . One thing led to another, and HUD said, 'Oh, by the way, you . . . haven't been conducting your business prudently and here's a letter of default.'" Lapp also recalls that so many problems existed between The Woodlands Development Corporation and HUD when he assumed control of relations that "it's a wonder they [HUD] did not take over this project." HUD did not do so, Lapp reasons,

14. Otto G. Stolz to Woodlands Development Corporation, ca. February 14–March 13, 1975. The total amount exceeded $17 million. Booz-Allen, *New Communities*, H-III-13.

because they handled the situation even more poorly than we did. They were a new organization also and they were having so many problems with so many other projects that we were able to keep going in spite of the fact that we had not followed many of our obligations, whether our statutory obligations or our Agreement obligations. Our reporting was terrible, the distinction between The Woodlands Development Corporation and other corporations was terrible, just as the human relations between the two agencies were terrible.[15]

Lapp's unraveling of the complicated intercompany transactions and HUD's uncustomary alacrity and attention to detail, perhaps, as Lapp suggests, because of its desire to help keep The Woodlands afloat, wrought satisfactory cure of the defaults by March 14, 1975.[16] While the exact cure for each infraction varied depending on its nature, in general each required that subsidiary organizations be kept in an "arm's-length" relationship with The Woodlands Development Corporation except for the Community Development and Construction Corporation, which could no longer be used as either a contractor or an agent in future land development. Also in each instance The Woodlands Development Corporation was required to institute improved management of its affairs, including various financial controls designed to ensure the expenditure of its funds only for its projects as provided for by the Project Agreement.[17]

The choice of Robinson Lapp to conduct relations with HUD eventually proved to be a fortunate one for The Woodlands Development Corporation. Nonetheless, long-standing mutual feelings of distrust, incompetency, negligence, and failure to meet moral, if not statutory, obligations lingered and continued to add to The Woodlands' financial straits. Three related issues in particular contributed to ongoing tensions and conflicts: equity contributions to The Woodlands Development Corporation by Mitchell and/or the parent company, the value of the 17,460 acres conveyed by Mitchell Development Corporation of the Southwest to The Woodlands Development Corporation in August, 1972, and HUD's failure to provide Title I grant funds to The Woodlands.

The Project Agreement required The Woodlands Development Corporation to grant a first lien on the 17,460 acres intended for development as The Woodlands to Chase Manhattan Bank as trustee for HUD

15. Interview with Robinson G. Lapp, February 23, 1981.
16. Otto G. Stolz to Woodlands Development Corporation, March 14, 1975, WDC Papers.
17. Otto G. Stolz to Woodlands Development Corporation, ca. February 14–March 13, 1975, WDC Papers.

and the debenture holders. The agreement also compelled The Woodlands Development Corporation to maintain landholdings having a market value equal to 110 percent of the principal amount of the debentures outstanding at any given time.[18] Since the schedule for retirement of the debentures did not commence until August 1, 1983, The Woodlands Development Corporation technically had to hold land valued at $55 million until that date. However, under a free-release clause in the Project Agreement, as The Woodlands Development Corporation expended funds to improve a development tract, the security value of the land in the nearest development area increased dollar for dollar by the amount spent. In this way, as the town developed, The Woodlands Development Corporation accrued credits allowing future releases of land from lien without payment of release prices. Both HUD and The Woodlands Development Corporation could demand a reappraisal of the unreleased land but could do so no more than once every two years.[19]

In late 1974 a financial shortfall forced The Woodlands Development Corporation to request a reappraisal in the hope of releasing additional land to be used as collateral for a $15 million loan. HUD, deeply concerned by this time about the solvency of The Woodlands Development Corporation and fearful that as financial manager it was overexposed in the event of a Woodlands Development Corporation bankruptcy, began insisting that The Woodlands Development Corporation was undersecured. The resultant reappraisals, three in all, satisfied neither HUD nor The Woodlands Development Corporation. In fact, HUD subsequently chose not to disclose the figure it preferred to accept but "hinted" at a value of approximately $40 million. This low appraisal denied The Woodlands Development Corporation an opportunity to release lands for additional borrowing.[20]

The matter of $10,001,030 of equity contribution provided for in the Project Agreement posed yet another subject of contention between HUD and The Woodlands Development Corporation. As previously noted, in August, 1972, Mitchell Development Corporation of the Southwest, a wholly owned subsidiary of Mitchell Energy and Development Corporation, conveyed 17,460 acres of land intended for development as The Woodlands to The Woodlands Development Corporation for the appraised value of $50,100,000. The Woodlands Development Cor-

18. Project Agreement, p. 51; R. N. Hinton to Edward Lee, November 28, 1977, WDC Papers.
19. Project Agreement, pp. 53–54.
20. Interview with Robinson G. Lapp, February 23, 1981; R. N. Hinton to Edward Lee, November 28, 1977, WDC Papers.

poration paid for the land with a $20,146,000 note subordinated to the federally guaranteed debentures and assumed $23,077,000 in mortgages and option payments. The Woodlands Development Corporation considered the remaining $6,777,100 to be an equity contribution by Mitchell Development Corporation of the Southwest. HUD, however, argued that the equity contribution amounted to only $2,243,000 because the $6,777,100 represented an intercompany appreciation of value, not the market value. HUD therefore demanded that the cash total be raised to the required amount.[21]

The third continuing point of conflict between HUD and The Woodlands Development Corporation — HUD's failure to provide promised grants amounting to $33 million over the twenty-year life of the project — further strained relations and significantly contributed to the corporation's financial difficulties. The gravity of this omission caused Mitchell to apply pressure on HUD through the Texas congressional delegation during the spring of 1975. One member of the delegation subsequently reported that he had discussed the problem with HUD Secretary Carla Hills and one person on her staff. "I did not," he wrote, "get too much encouragement from HUD officials, but I am inclined to feel the situation may not be too bad."[22] One week later Robinson Lapp informed Mitchell and other corporate officers that chances for a large grant looked promising. "I was told confidentially," Lapp reported, "that our efforts through Texas Senators and Congressmen to press this matter with Mrs. Hills had had a significant influence."[23] Lapp's optimistic appraisal proved at least partly correct as HUD broke with its previous policy of barring The Woodlands from Title I grants to provide funds totaling $2,840,000 during the remainder of 1975.[24]

Something of a climax to the controversies revolving around the three outstanding issues came in a roundabout fashion. In October, 1975, HUD informed The Woodlands Development Corporation that the company's extension in January, 1975, of timber-cutting rights sold in May, 1969, to Louisiana-Pacific Corporation included lands under indenture and therefore constituted a default.[25] In fact, however, and contrary to HUD's interpretation, at the time of the land conveyance

21. R. N. Hinton to Edward Lee, November 28, 1977, WDC Papers; interview with Robinson G. Lapp, February 23, 1981; Booz-Allen, *New Communities,* H-IV-16, H-IV-26.

22. Cong. George Mahon to H. J. Blanchard, April 18, 1975, WDC Papers.

23. Robinson G. Lapp to G. P. Mitchell; Bernard F. Clark; Leland W. Carter; William Tonery; Lawrence S. Kash; Robert N. Hinton, Jr.; Richard P. Browne; and J. Michael Kilgore, April 25, 1975, WDC Papers.

24. "Fact Sheet, The Woodlands New Town," July 7, 1980, WDC Papers.

25. Secretary, HUD, to Robinson G. Lapp, October 1, 1975, WDC Papers.

from Mitchell Development Corporation of the Southwest to The Woodlands Development Corporation the contract provided that the former company retained its right to the proceeds from the timber sales. HUD's adamant insistence that the proceeds go to The Woodlands Development Corporation, plus its continuing demands for increased equity contributions and the ominous threat of default inherent in the low appraisal of the corporation's lands, forced a resolution in March, 1976.[26]

On March 12, 1976, HUD, The Woodlands Development Corporation, Mitchell Energy and Development Corporation, and Mitchell Development Corporation of the Southwest executed a Letter of Agreement which modified some of the terms of the Project Agreement and the indenture (the mortgage instrument securing payment of the debentures and performance of the Project Agreement). Under this new pact affiliates of The Woodlands Development Corporation — that is, wholly owned subsidiaries of Mitchell Energy and Development Corporation and Mitchell Development Corporation of the Southwest — agreed to execute promissory notes payable to The Woodlands Development Corporation secured by mortgages on land and structures they held in The Woodlands. In addition The Woodlands Development Corporation agreed to mortgage some of its finished lots, some cash and notes receivable, and all of its personal property. These notes and mortgages were then deposited with Chase Manhattan Bank, as trustee, to secure payment of the debentures.

The Letter of Agreement also set aside the free-release feature of the Project Agreement by requiring The Woodlands Development Corporation to pay $14,609 an acre for undeveloped land released from lien. Those funds were placed in an escrow account called the "land-release account." In this fashion funds in the land-release account provided substitute security for raw land released for development. The agreement provided for a continuation of this process until an undetermined future date when a reappraisal showed a property value of at least $55 million.[27]

Although the March Letter of Agreement provided greater security for the debentures, the arrangement satisfied neither HUD nor The Woodlands Development Corporation. HUD continued to demand larger infusions of capital to guard against any contingency during the

---

26. Interview with Robinson G. Lapp, February 23, 1981. Lapp informed a superior: "I cannot overstate our need to work out at least a one-year business plan with HUD. We may be in default over financial covenants before February ends, unless we come to an agreement." Robinson G. Lapp to J. Leonard Rogers, February 2, 1976, WDC Papers.

27. R. N. Hinton to Edward Lee, November 28, 1977, WDC Papers.

89

life of the debentures. At the same time The Woodlands Development Corporation insisted on a higher property appraisal or, failing that, negotiation of a year-to-year working agreement reducing the amount paid for land releases to give the company greater financial flexibility.

The resultant stalemate ended with a new agreement on February 1, 1977, the Annual Budget Control Document (ABCD). An annually negotiated agreement expiring on January 31 unless renewed, the ABCD required The Woodlands Development Corporation to submit a one-year budget for the fiscal year to HUD indicating expected sources of revenues and proposed expenditures. It also required, for information purposes only, submission of a quarterly budget for the following year and an annual budget for each year thereafter through the life of the project. Any activity pursued by the company involving the expenditure of funds not specifically described in the annual budget or agreed to in advance by HUD constituted a default.

The ABCD further compelled Mitchell Energy and Development Corporation to contribute a minimum of $3,639,000 in equity or subordinated debt to The Woodlands Development Corporation during the fiscal year ending January 31, 1978. In turn, HUD committed itself to provide grants up to $2,789,000 plus a so-called incentive grant of $850,000 if the company met prescribed performance tests. In the event that The Woodlands Development Corporation failed to meet the performance test, it forfeited part or all of the "incentive grant."

Finally, the ABCD reduced the release price for undeveloped land to $8,000 an acre. These funds were combined with money previously paid into the Land Release Account and placed in an "Additional Sinking Fund" retained by the trustee as security for the debentures and for their retirement as scheduled under the Project Agreement:

Year	Fund Amount
1983	$1,500,000
1984	1,500,000
1985	2,000,000
1986	2,000,000
1987	3,000,000
1988	4,500,000
1989	6,000,000
1990	7,500,000
1991	9,500,000
1992	Balance ($13,500,000)[28]

28. Ibid.

Relations between the company and HUD improved during the years after 1977 and the first ABCD. HUD began providing larger grants, and the reorganization of The Woodlands Development Corporation began paying dividends in the form of timely, accurate reports and effective cost control.[29] The question of a fair appraisal of company properties, however, was not resolved until the winter of 1979–80. At that time, according to Lapp, HUD received an appraisal of $150 million, which it then attempted to suppress. When informed that the company knew of the appraised value, HUD had no alternative but to order a new appraisal, which placed the value at approximately $75 million.[30]

These events, at least in Lapp's perspective, marked the "turning point where we were no longer the ones with our necks down on the ground and their [HUD's] feet on us—we were much more in an agency-to-agency bargaining position, and it's been a much more equitable thing since then."[31] Improved relations did not, however, result in anything like a second honeymoon. HUD continued to insist on payment for land releases and persistently complained about the corporation's failure to provide low- and moderate-income housing as well as the "Waspish" image projected by The Woodlands. One HUD official, after touring the new town and some nearby competing projects in the summer of 1977, commented: "I sincerely believe that you offer a superior project *and* living environment. . . . I noted, however, with considerable regret, that The Woodlands has attracted a very small number of minority persons."[32]

To add to the burdens shouldered by Mitchell and his revamped management group, the city of Conroe, always a bit leery of the newcomer in the area, participated in—if it did not initiate—a renewal of the old controversy over jurisdiction of The Woodlands. During 1966, Conroe had extended its extraterritorial jurisdiction southward along I-45 and westward along FM 1488 in a strip annexation which included part of The Woodlands. Following the 1971 minidebate spurred by The Woodlands' successful request to be included in Houston's extraterri-

29 Title I grants awarded to The Woodlands Development Corporation by HUD amounted to $5,480,300 in 1976, $5,010,000 in 1977, and $2,518,000 in 1979. "Fact Sheet, The Woodlands New Town," July 7, 1980, WDC Papers.

30. Interview with Robinson G. Lapp, February 23, 1981.

31. Ibid.

32. Gail Ettinger to Robinson G. Lapp, August 5, 1977, WDC Papers. Lapp earlier described HUD's increasing tendency to interfere in the management of The Woodlands and its "hysteria about mid-range and low- and moderate-income housing." Robinson G. Lapp to J. Leonard Rogers, September 3, 1976, WDC Papers.

torial jurisdiction, The Woodlands Development Corporation, to sat-
isfy HUD's desire that no conflicting jurisdictions be present in the new
town, requested in December, 1972, that Conroe relinquish its hold
on land in The Woodlands.[33] Conroe's Mayor Mickey Deison emphatically refused and informed the company's attorney: "We are unalter-
ably opposed to any encroachment by Houston [into] Conroe's extraterritorial jurisdiction. We have no intention of waiving our rights."
Subsequent discussions between Deison and Houston's Mayor Louie
Welch brought no resolution.[34]

In May, 1973, the Houston City Council, in a move designed to
block any additions by Conroe, approved an ordinance of extension
of Houston's extraterritorial jurisdiction but excluded "any lands or ter-
ritory presently included within the extraterritorial jurisdiction of any
city, town, or village." The ordinance also provided that The Woodlands Development Corporation would pay the cost of any litigation
resulting from the extension. The issue remained stalemated until February 12, 1974, when Conroe gave its permission to a group of citizens
residing within its alleged jurisdiction to incorporate as the city of Shenandoah. The would-be incorporators then claimed grandiose boundaries embracing much of The Woodlands, including the site of the Metro
Center. The loss of developer control of The Woodlands, not to mention potential tax revenues if Shenandoah succeeded in its plans, posed
an intolerable threat to The Woodlands Development Corporation. The
company therefore spared no effort to thwart Shenandoah's designs.
Before the scheduled citizens' vote on incorporation Robert Burns, of
the noted Houston law firm of Sears and Burns, informed a meeting
of Shenandoah residents that gaps in Conroe's strip annexation rendered its extension invalid. The voters, obviously unswayed by legal
niceties, voted on March 16, 1974, to incorporate with the previously
drawn boundaries.[35]

For several months following Shenandoah's incorporation the issue faded from public notice while representatives of The Woodlands
and the three cities attempted to negotiate a compromise. During the
sessions The Woodlands' attorneys unsuccessfully attempted to obtain
a three-point solution providing that (1) Shenandoah deannex lands

33. Alan F. Levin to Fred Hofheinz, April 14, 1975, WDC Papers.
34. "The Woodlands Chronicle" (manuscript in WDC Papers), p. 84. Deison had
earlier commented during a meeting of Conroe's city planning commission that the people of Conroe were skeptical about the new town and that since they "were there first
. . . they expected to have their say." "Woodlands Village Chronicle," September 19,
1972.
35. Alan F. Levin to Fred Hofheinz, April 14, 1975, WDC Papers.

in The Woodlands, (2) The Woodlands compensate Shenandoah by providing the city with free police and fire protection as well as water and sewer service; and (3) Conroe and Houston agree to an apportionment of the area in which future jurisdictional conflicts might occur.

Rebuffed in its attempts to attain an equitable agreement, The Woodlands Development Corporation drew some renewed hope from a July, 1974, opinion by the city of Houston's planning department, after a reexamination of Conroe's strip annexations, that "these dimensional gaps are serious enough to probably render the ordinances faulty if attacked in court."[36] At this point, however, the company chose not to institute a legal suit and continued to pursue a compromise. In September, 1974, The Woodlands Development Corporation again proposed that Conroe and Shenandoah agree to cede their claims to lands in The Woodlands and Houston and Conroe apportion the remaining area. The proposal also repeated the offer of provision of police and fire protection and added offers of use of The Woodlands park planning services, construction of a road linking Shenandoah with The Woodlands, and provision of a second highway exit for Shenandoah by extension of the existing access road. Shenandoah's city council rejected the offer because "the land they were wanting us to give up is worth some $20 million. . . . The tax revenue would be fantastic." When asked by The Woodlands Development Corporation officials to make a counterproposal, the council submitted a long list of the city's "needs" over the next twenty years, including police cars, fire-fighting equipment, and a 100-foot greenbelt between Shenandoah and The Woodlands complete with trails and picnic tables. "We knew," Shenandoah Mayor Roger B. Davis later explained, "we wouldn't get nearly what we asked for. . . . We just provided a list to negotiate on. They started on the low side and we started on the high side."[37]

Exasperated and convinced by this time of the futility of further negotiations, Burns recommended in February, 1975, that The Woodlands try to persuade Houston to initiate legal proceedings. In the absence of such action, Burns warned, "I can give no assurances that the Shenandoah gangrene can be excised."[38] In April, 1975, the Houston City Council voted to authorize the city's legal department to institute legal action to protect Houston's extraterritorial jurisdiction. Almost a year later the prolonged issue reached an anticlimactic out-of-court settlement by which the cities of Houston and Conroe agreed to rec-

---

36. Ibid.
37. *Conroe Daily Courier*, May 1, 1975.
38. Robert L. Burns to Robert N. Hinton, February 4, 1975, WDC Papers.

ognize Shenandoah's status as an incorporated city. In return, Shenandoah agreed to deannex land in The Woodlands claimed by Houston through the May, 1973, extension of its extraterritorial jurisdiction.[39]

The frustrations forced on him by successive financial and political crises during the first years of The Woodlands' existence undoubtedly cost George Mitchell many anxious moments. His unflagging dedication to the project plus the monetary resources of Mitchell Energy and Development Corporation sustained him through those tense times and ensured ultimate success. One key victory, however, an essential component of the new town as a place where its residents could work, play, and learn—the establishment of a university campus at The Woodlands—continued to evade him despite every effort.

As previously noted, on March 7, 1972, the University of Houston's Board of Regents accepted Mitchell's offer to donate four hundred acres of land in The Woodlands as a site for a north campus. In making his offer, Mitchell pointed out that because of the seemingly unlimited and expanding nature of higher education in the 1960s the university's central campus would soon be overcrowded and had only limited space for future expansion. The new town, with its available acreage and its projected population of 250,000 within a twenty-mile radius, was an obvious solution to these problems.[40]

Mitchell's linking of his new town to the advantages it offered higher education was not entirely altruistic. The Gladstone group's report projected, within twelve years after its opening, a new-town campus of fifteen thousand students supported by two thousand faculty and staff. The presence of the university community would create an additional housing demand of approximately four thousand units for faculty, staff, and students who chose to live near the campus. In addition, an annual $14 million of retail spending would be generated as a direct impact of the campus.[41]

Mitchell's plans for a university campus happily coincided with the aspirations of the University of Houston administration. In 1968 the Coordinating Board of the Texas College and University System had recommended the establishment of two new University of Houston–administered campuses in the metropolitan area. One was to be an upper-level institution with junior, senior, and graduate courses. This

39. *Houston Chronicle,* May 1, 1975; Robert L. Burns to Roscoe Jones, March 17, 1976, WDC Papers.
40. Interview with George P. Mitchell, October 16, 1979. Also helpful on the general background of The Woodlands campus were interview with Charles Kelly, August 31, 1982; interview with Coulson Tough, August 31, 1982.
41. Gladstone Associates, Development Program, pp. 103–109.

eventually became the University of Houston Clear Lake Campus. The other projected new campus was to offer a traditional four-year undergraduate program and could also offer a one-year graduate program leading to a master of arts degree. Following acceptance of Mitchell's donation of land, the University of Houston's administration chose to assume that the second campus would be situated in The Woodlands. They therefore began formulating plans for the new campus and tried to secure the coordinating board's final approval, which would be necessary to obtain legislative funding.[42] University officials targeted 1977 for the beginning of campus construction and planned for classes to begin one year later.

In the summer of 1974, however, the situation drastically changed, largely because of another move by the university administration. In August, 1974, the university purchased the downtown Houston building formerly occupied by South Texas Junior College and announced its intention to operate the school as a separate campus. The purchase came as a surprise to the university's central-campus community, and a faculty governance organization later expressed its concern over the lack of faculty consultation. Rumor explained President Hoffman's precipitous action as being necessary to prevent purchase of the junior college by another university in the state system.[43]

Although the coordinating board eventually approved the acquisition of the Downtown Campus, a staff report insisted that the purchase fullfilled the board's 1968 recommendation for the establishment of two additional University of Houston campuses, i.e., the Clear Lake and Downtown units. To worsen matters, Texas Commissioner of Higher Education Kenneth Ashworth announced that he supported the position taken in the staff report. A university administrator reacted to publication of the staff report's stance with expressions of "dismay" because it put approval of The Woodlands campus in considerable jeopardy.[44]

A contingent of university officials led by President Hoffman appeared before the program development committee of the coordinating board to attempt refutation of the staff report's contention. Hoffman argued that the Downtown Campus was intended to be not a "new" undertaking but merely a continuation of the old University Downtown School, where off-campus courses had been taught in rented facilities for many years. He again pointed out the great potential of the

42. *Houston Post,* July 24, 1976.
43. Ibid., April 25, 1979.
44. Ibid., July 24, December 2, 1976.

proposed campus in The Woodlands and the growing population base it would serve. As he concluded his remarks, Hoffman announced a change in the educational program to be offered at The Woodlands campus. The proposed school, Hoffman informed the committee members, would offer only upper-level (junior, senior, and graduate) instruction. A newspaper reporter covering the meeting noted that the altered program apparently was a "goodwill gesture" intended to appease a local community college which feared competition from a campus in The Woodlands. Although several committee members voiced their support of Hoffman, one member criticized the circumstances of the Downtown Campus acquisition, and another expressed concern over the considerable expense involved in establishing a campus in The Woodlands.[45]

Early in 1977 the program development committee met again to deliberate on the proposal. President Hoffman reiterated his plea for approval on the basis of population growth in the area and potential student enrollment. He also called the committee's attention to the value of Mitchell's gift of four hundred acres for the campus site—a site worth approximately $10 million and likely to appreciate rapidly as The Woodlands developed. He urged the coordinating board to approve the project even if actual construction of the campus was delayed until 1980 or 1982 because it was "an outstanding opportunity to acquire a fine property for a needed and worthwhile purpose."

Commissioner Ashworth emphatically disagreed with Hoffman's claims concerning the population growth and potential of the northern Harris–southern Montgomery County area. Ashworth's growth projection indicated that the area would not reach a 200,000 population within a ten-mile radius by 1990 and thus could not support a campus of 15,000 students. Furthermore, Ashworth argued, a campus in The Woodlands was unnecessary because of existing educational facilities serving the area. There were nineteen colleges and universities within fifty miles of The Woodlands, including six publicly supported senior colleges and six publicly supported junior colleges. The public colleges, Ashworth asserted, would be injured by The Woodlands campus, particularly the two nearest ones, Sam Houston State University and Prairie View A&M University. Each school had an enrollment well under its 12,000 capacity.

While Ashworth urged the committee to deny a recommendation for the establishment of The Woodlands campus, he also expressed his willingness to reconsider his position if certain conditions were met.

45. Ibid., October 15, 1976.

Those conditions were that the Harris-Montgomery county area attain a population of 200,000 within a ten-mile radius of the proposed campus; that the nearest senior college, Sam Houston State University, at Huntsville, reach an enrollment of 12,000 students; and that The Woodlands campus offer only upper-level instruction.

The program development committee recommended against authorization of The Woodlands campus. At a subsequent meeting of the full coordinating board, the members denied approval by a vote of 10 to 5 and did not officially recognize the conditions suggested by Commissioner Ashworth. As a newspaper reporter put it, "The motion [of the board] cast aside the conditions Ashworth recommended and simply called for denial of authorization . . . period."[46]

Undoubtedly President Hoffman and other university officials were bitterly disappointed by the large vote for denial. Hoffman later indicated, however, that The Woodlands proposal would be resubmitted when Ashworth's conditions had been met. He also predicted that in the future "members of the board [will] feel it will be needed. It was just a matter of timing with some of them."[47] George Mitchell remained equally optimistic and stated: "We and the university believe this campus is important to the state and to Houston. If Houston is going to have four and a half million people, it is urgent."[48]

The reasons for the failure of the coordinating board to authorize The Woodlands campus are complex. By late 1976 public officials began to have second thoughts about the skyrocketing costs of higher education in Texas. Commenting that "it could break us all," Gov. Dolph Briscoe noted that state expenditures for higher education had increased 30 percent in each of the three bienniums previous to 1977 and that the projected budget for the biennium beginning in 1979 called for a 52 percent increase. Such an increase meant higher-education costs of over $3 billion of a state budget of $12 billion. Commissioner Ashworth, Lt. Gov. Bill Hobby, and Texas House Speaker Billy Clayton also indicated that it was time to reduce drastically the expenditures for education.[49]

Concern about rising educational costs unquestionably influenced the decision of the coordinating board to deny authorization of The Woodlands campus. One board member, Robert P. Teague, Sr., of Texas City, stated that, while he favored the campus in principle, he was re-

46. Ibid., January 26, 27, 1977.
47. Ibid., July 7, 1977.
48. Ibid.
49. Ibid., December 1, 1976.

luctant to approve it because "it's only overnight before they [university administrators] are back asking you for money."[50]

Influential political leaders in the Texas legislature also opposed establishment of The Woodlands campus. State Senator William T. Moore, "a bitter foe of The Woodlands campus plan,"[51] represented the interests of Texas A&M University and Sam Houston State University. He believed that the campus could not be justified and that it posed a threat to his constituents. State Representative Jimmie C. Edwards of Conroe, whose district included the Huntsville area, also opposed the campus, as did State Senator Payton McKnight, chairman of the Senate State Affairs Committee. These legislative leaders, all having substantial seniority, undoubtedly did not refrain from imparting their views to members of the coordinating board.

The administration of the University of Houston must also share a large part of the responsibility for failure to win approval of The Woodlands campus. The precipitate acquisition of the Downtown Campus was a strategic error which placed the university on the defensive in its dealings with the coordinating board. Also, the statistical brief prepared by the university's staff to support need for the campus was weak. Ashworth's brief rebutting the university's stance was stronger and more accurate. Subsequent acceptance of Ashworth's conditions by university officials validated the relevance of his statistics. In short, the university had not adequately prepared its homework.

Throughout the summer and early fall of 1977 university officials met frequently with The Woodlands staff to develop plans for resubmission of the campus proposal to the coordinating board. Both Mitchell and Hoffman affirmed their dedication to the project and voiced optimism that with careful preparation the campus would soon be approved.[52] But in the late fall of 1977 the University of Houston incurred national notoriety in the revelation of widespread frauds involving over $15 million of its security investments. The subsequent investigations and litigation resulting from those irregularities lasted well over two years, and, although only one university official was directly involved in the frauds, the end result tended to stigmatize the entire university administration. The fraud, and the ensuing pall which hung over the university, undoubtedly contributed to the decision to hold resubmission in abeyance for several years.

University officials did not consider it feasible to announce plans

50. Ibid., February 24, 1977.
51. Ibid., January 26, 1977.
52. Ibid., July 7, 1977.

to seek coordinating board approval of The Woodlands campus until the summer of 1982. Led by the new president, Charles E. Bishop, university administrators met with various state officials preparatory to submission of a new proposal to the board. President Bishop presented an impressive eighty-six-page brief in support of the need for a campus. He argued that the conditions set forth previously by Commissioner Ashworth had been substantially met and that the burgeoning growth of the northern Harris–southern Montgomery County area fully justified a university campus in The Woodlands.[53]

But problems remained. When informed of the university's resubmission of its request, Commissioner Ashworth stated that, while he would evaluate the supporting evidence before making a recommendation to the coordinating board, he would "start from a position of being extremely skeptical that it [The Woodlands campus] is needed."[54]

As of this writing, the fate of George Mitchell's long quest to obtain a campus of the University of Houston in The Woodlands remains questionable, particularly in view of an uncertain state economy. Yet several factors enhance the likelihood of eventual success. The university administration and The Woodlands staff are more fully prepared to support the need for a campus. Several important legislative foes of the proposal no longer serve, and the personnel of the coordinating board has greatly changed. Above all, continued population growth in The Woodlands area may well be the determining factor in the eventual establishment of the University of Houston campus in The Woodlands.

53. Ibid., August 25, 1982.
54. Ibid., August 8, 1982.

7. Building a New Town

THE CORNERSTONES OF COMMUNITY

The difficult two years following the grand opening of The Woodlands in October, 1974, witnessed a near stagnation of progressive activity in the new town. J. Leonard Rogers, a Canadian-born certified public accountant and a veteran of community development in La Jolla, California, recalls that when he took over as vice-president and general manager of The Woodlands Development Corporation in late 1975, construction had ground to a halt, and employee morale fluctuated from low to zero. Rogers says:

> For the first year or so we just really worked on building up morale because it had been completely turned off. . . . We had to get engineering and master facilities started. The East golf course had not been built — drainage had not been installed on the entire east side. And so we started, . . . but it was the summer of 1976 before we really got turned around. The installation of a drainage system on the east side was the milestone that enabled us to start construction again because without predraining it is impossible to do anything in The Woodlands.[1]

In the interim, although the volume of new-home sales gave some cause for optimism, a general sense of gloom pervaded the few business establishments operating in The Wharf shopping mall. In August, 1975, in the words of one shop owner, "Activity just died. It was as if

100   1. Interview with J. Leonard Rogers, October 31, 1984.

someone had put out a sign that said 'Do Not Enter.'" The beleaguered store owners stressed the urgent need for the addition of a previously projected supermarket and a twin cinema to attract potential customers. All the business owners, though exasperated and discouraged by lack of commercial development and business stagnation, nonetheless expressed their intention to persevere because "within a year or two this will be *the* mall to be in."[2]

An executive in charge of new-home and lot sales for The Woodlands Realty Company, a subsidiary of Mitchell Energy and Development Corporation, observed early in 1975 that HUD had expressed unhappiness with lagging new home sales and concern about constant employee cutbacks. "We've made some mistakes here," he added. "We haven't attracted the industry we hoped to in order to bring people in here. We solicited industry all over the country when perhaps we should have concentrated on the local people who already know about our country club and our golf course and whose executives and employees would like to live close to their work."[3]

A few bright spots did exist, however, in the general gloom of 1975. New-home and lot sales accelerated during the summer. Also, the addition of three home-building firms, including Centennial Homes, a subsidiary of the Weyerhaeuser Company, brought to sixteen the total number of builders operating in The Woodlands. During the year contractors completed 251 single-family detached homes and began construction on 90 more, and realtors found purchasers for a total of 287. Newcomers demanding apartment and townhouse units brought the new town's population to nearly 900 by year's end.[4]

The following year brought more rapid growth. During 1976 new-home sales dramatically increased from the previous year's 287 to 773, while lots sold or under contract rose from 883 in 1975 to 1,091. Completion of an $8.5 million high school, J. L. McCullough Senior High School, on a 50-acre site increased to three the number of schools in The Woodlands, and total population rose to nearly 2,200. Further advances included the purchase of a 26-acre site in the Trade Center by Jack Eckerd Corporation for construction of a 280,000-square-foot rail-served distribution center, plus the leasing of office, commercial, and industrial space to several firms, including Continental Oil Company, Peerless Engineering Company, and Texaco, Inc.[5]

2. *Conroe Daily Courier,* January 28, 1976.

3. Ibid.

4. Mitchell Energy and Development Corporation, Annual Report, Year Ended January 31, 1976, pp. 15–16; *Woodlands Villager,* May 24, 1978.

5. *Houston Business Journal,* August 23, 1976; The Woodlands Development Cor-

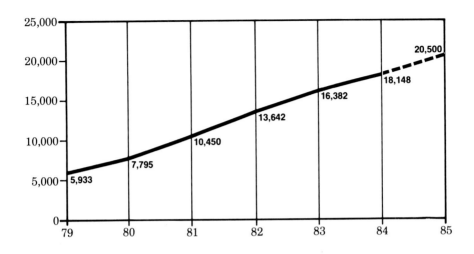

25,000
20,500
20,000
18,148
15,000
16,382
13,642
10,000
10,450
7,795
5,000 5,933
0
79   80   81   82   83   84   85

Fiscal Year Ended January 31

The Woodlands population.

Progress made during 1975–76 continued in succeeding years. Total population reached 4,100 in 1977, 5,900 in 1978, 8,000 in 1979, 10,450 in 1980, 13,640 in 1981, 16,380 in 1982, 18,150 in 1983, and 18,733 in 1984.[6] The steady if unspectacular population growth in The Woodlands from 1977 through 1984 stemmed from several factors. As noted by J. Leonard Rogers, the installation of a drainage system in the area east of Lake Harrison plus acquisition of $9 million in permanent financing from Equitable Life Assurance Society of the United States and a $7.5 million reimbursement from MUD No. 6 permitted completion of the second eighteen-hole golf course in the fall of 1977 and an increased pace in land development and construction. As an example of the latter, another milestone came with the opening in the fall of 1978 of Jamail's of The Woodlands, a 28,000-square-foot supermarket adjacent to The Wharf shopping mall. Edward P. Lee, president of The Woodlands Development Corporation, believes that the arrival of a

poration, News Release, April, 1977; Mitchell Energy and Development Corporation, Annual Report, Year Ended January 31, 1977, pp. 21–22.

6. *Woodlands Villager,* March 8, 1978, February 25, 1981; Mitchell Energy and Development Corporation, Annual Report, Year Ended January 31, 1978, p. 23; Annual Report, Year Ended January 31, 1979, p. 4; Annual Report, Year Ended January 31, 1980, p. 24; Annual Report, Year Ended January 31, 1983, p. 21; Annual Report, Year Ended January 31, 1984, p. 17; Annual Report, Year Ended January 31, 1985, p. 25.

PRIOR RESIDENCE	1978	1983
■ Local Area	32%	33%
■ Houston Area	31%	35%
■ Other	37%	32%
REASON FOR MOVE		
■ Job	43%	40%
■ 1st Home Buyer	22%	29%
■ Move Up	20%	15%
EMPLOYMENT		
■ Local Area	35%	50%
■ CBD	26%	20%

The Woodlands new home buyer profile.

supermarket marked a turnaround in the development of a sense of community in The Woodlands because until then residents had few if any centers where they could gather with their neighbors. "It became almost a social experience for people to go to the market to meet their neighbors," Lee said. "People wanted to be seen and see who was there. That same pattern continues to this day as our village centers are being opened. People take a great deal of comfort from the sense of belonging to a community."[7]

The ever-increasing visibility of The Woodlands, both locally and internationally, also contributed to steadily increasing home sales and general development. The wooded, natural environment and recreational amenities offered by the new town, combined with a more sophisticated advertising campaign downplaying an earlier, not entirely intended implication of utopia and instead stressing The Woodlands

7. *Houston Post,* November 6, 1975; Mitchell Energy and Development Corporation, Annual Report, Year Ended January 31, 1976, p. 17; *Woodlands Villager,* September 27, 1978; interview with Edward P. Lee and Randall L. Woods, October 31, 1984.   **103**

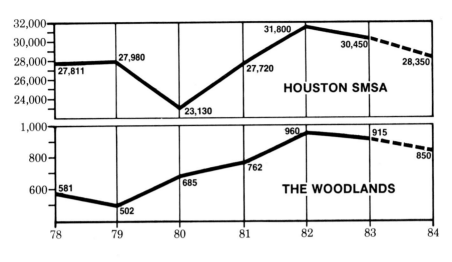

Source: National Association of Home Builders and
The Woodlands Corporation

Single-family housing starts, Houston Standard Metropolitan Statistical Area and The Woodlands.

as a place to live, work, and play, significantly contributed to growth. In the words of a record-setting residential-home salesman: "One reason I can sell is because I am sold on the product. George Mitchell had the foresight to construct the amenities before selling lots and houses." Or, as a successful homebuilder explained on the occasion of announcing his company's intent to double its production of the previous year: "The demand is so great . . . that our company must expand. Our homes are sold even before the framework is finished."[8]

Without question the attention and careful planning given to the construction of recreational facilities in the new town, plus the successful selling of the quality of those amenities, constituted a major factor in the heightened visibility of The Woodlands. Before beginning construction of the first eighteen-hole golf course, The Woodlands Development Corporation named Joseph L. Lee and Joseph S. Finger as designers. Both possessed eminent qualifications. Lee, the principal designer, had previously planned or renovated more than three hundred golf courses in the United States and abroad, including the Professional Golf Association's National Golf Course. Finger, a Houston-based, internationally known golf-course architect, acted as project consultant

8. The Woodlands Development Corporation, news releases, April 27, 1977, February 1, 1978.

104

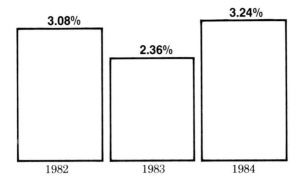

3.08% 2.36% 3.24%

1982   1983   1984

Note: Based on The Woodlands sales compared to regional starts.

Single-family housing, The Woodlands' capture of the Houston area.

and area specialist. In September, 1974, Carlton Gipson joined the design team as vice-president of golf management and grounds maintenance for The Woodlands Development Corporation. Gipson, a graduate in agronomy from Texas A&M University, had formerly served as superintendent of courses at Cherry Hills Country Club, in Denver, Colorado, and the Mexico City Country Club and as a director of the Golf Course Superintendents' Association of America.

Construction of the eighteen-hole, 7,010-yard course entailed, in addition to clearing and grading, the removal of 300,000 yards of earth to form lakes and ponds and to build tees, fairways, and greens. To ensure championship quality, Gipson shipped in white silica sand from Whales Lake, Florida, for use in the bunkers surrounding most of the greens. After a one-year search, in yet another effort to reinforce the emphasis on quality, The Woodlands Development Corporation named Doug Sanders, winner of some twenty Professional Golf Association tournaments, as director of golf. Sanders told Lawrence S. Kash, senior vice-president of building development and project director of the Commercial, Conference, and Leisure Center (CCLC), "What we really need for instant recognition is a major tournament . . . like the Houston Open." Sanders's advice, to the good fortune of The Woodlands, came when the Houston Open was falling on hard times and even into disrepute. The misfortunes besetting the tournament included yearly shifts of site after 1971; unfortunate scheduling, placing it between major tournaments in Fort Worth and Dallas; and alleged mismanagement. In May, 1974, the Houston Golf Association and The Woodlands De-

105

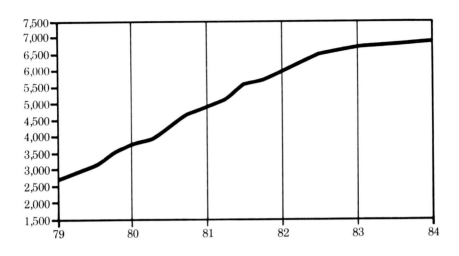

Source: The Woodlands Corporation.

The Woodlands, occupied dwelling units.

velopment Corporation agreed to a contract making The Woodlands the home of the Houston Open for the next ten years.[9]

Announcement of the agreement drew expressions of skepticism from most local sports columnists and open scorn from a Galveston-based writer. A Houston journalist responded to the new pact by observing that the Houston Open needed three things: a superior course, a different date, and the presence of a number of big-name professionals. "At the moment," he lamented, "prospects are bleak for realizing any of the three." Another metropolitan-area sportswriter expressed doubt that The Woodlands course could be ready by tournament time in 1975 and concluded, "The move will be good only if The Woodlands golf course is truly a championship layout and not one carved out between patios, kitchens and swimming pools." A Galveston scribe added the most biting commentary: "The plain fact is that the tournament doesn't have a home and is being used by developments which need the publicity to sell houses."[10]

Gipson, Kash, and Sanders concurred in doubting that the course

9. *Conroe Daily Courier*, December 24, 1972, September 12, 1972; *Texas Builders*, July, 1974; *Woodlands Sun*, September 11, 1974; *Houston Post*, May 12, May 31, 1974; *Houston Chronicle*, May 14, June 16, 1974; Galveston *Daily News*, May 19, 1974.

10. *Houston Post*, May 13, 1974; *Houston Chronicle*, May 14, 1974; *Galveston Daily News*, May 19, 1974.

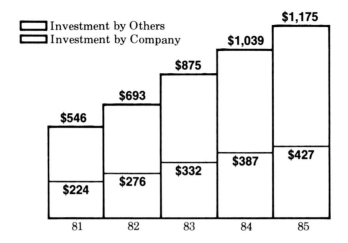

Fiscal Year Ended January 31

The Woodlands, cumulative capital invested.

would be in championship condition by May, 1975, pointing out that only twelve holes had been sprigged and acknowledging the normal need for more than one growing season for maximum playing conditions. Kash, who also served as a director of the Houston Golf Association, affirmed, on the other hand, the company's desire to provide a permanent home for the tournament and attempted beforehand to defuse allegations of solely mercenary motives on the developer's part. "It is not our intention," Kash asserted, "to have it [the tournament] a couple of years to sell homes . . . [and] then kick it out."[11]

The rousing success of the 1975 Houston Open, won by Bruce Crampton in a two-stroke victory over the then relatively unknown Dr. Gil Morgan, in a field including Ben Crenshaw, Ray Floyd, and John Mahaffey, ensured its permanency in The Woodlands. It also resulted in a return during the next year's tournament of national network television coverage, an increase in total prize money, and the presence of more high-prestige professionals, including Lee Trevino, Hubert

11. *Houston Post,* May 31, 1974. Another representative of The Woodlands Development Corporation commented two years later: "We intend to make this a really quality tournament. . . . We don't see it as a means to sell houses, but as a part of the fabric of the new town. The residents feel a part of it and it's an all volunteer army from the country club that makes the show a sucess." *Houston Chronicle,* August 12, 1976.

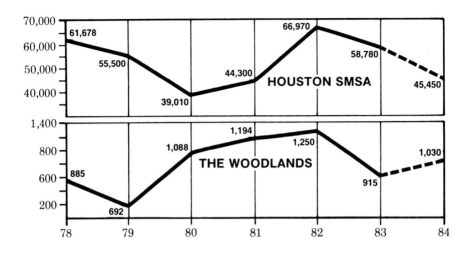

Total housing starts, Houston Standard Metropolitan Statistical Area and The Woodlands.

Green, and Lee Elder (the 1976 winner). Also in 1976 former University of Texas football coach Darrell Royal moved his popular pro-am celebrity invitational tournament from Galveston to The Woodlands — an annual event which attracted lustrous names of the likes of country singer Willie Nelson; comedians Bob Hope, Jackie Gleason, and Phyllis Diller; and motion-picture and television stars Robert Stack, Hugh O'Brian, and Fred MacMurray.[12]

Swimming and tennis facilities in the new town received emphasis equal to that given to golf courses. The Woodlands Swim and Athletic Center, completed in late 1974 and boosted as the "largest in the Southwest," included "every kind of swimming pool for every age and every area of expertise." The Swim Center's facilities included four individually heated swimming pools — three outdoors and one indoors — including an Olympic-size pool and an eighteen-foot-deep diving tank complete with a ten-meter diving tower and a "bubble machine" designed to form a softer cushion, or pillow, for divers; a gymnasium; eight outdoor tennis courts; and locker and kitchen areas. Intended primarily for the use of residents who chose to become members, the Swim Center's splendid facilities nonetheless unabashedly advertised the devel-

12. *Houston Post,* April 25, May 4, 1976; *Houston Chronicle,* June 5, 1976; *Woodlands Villager,* May 4, 1977, May 7, 1980.

oper's hopes that their quality would appeal to officials of national and international swimming and diving meets as they cast about for choice locales. Furthermore, to develop a local club capable of competing on national and international levels, The Woodlands Development Corporation chose Dick A. Smith as director of the Swim Center and later appointed Walter and Nancy Schleuter, of the nationally prestigious Multnomah Swim Club, of Portland, Oregon, as coaches. Smith's career as a champion collegiate diver and swimming-diving coach spanned forty years and the development of more than three hundred world-class swimmers and divers. His worldwide reputation, plus the quality facilities offered by the Swim Center, led to the selection of The Woodlands as the site of the 1975 Amateur Athletic Union Outdoor Diving Championships and the Pan American Diving Trials. During the next several years a number of equally prestigious competitions followed, including the first International Age Group Diving Competition, the Master's Diving Competition, and the First FINA World Diving Cup.[13]

The attraction of major tennis tournaments to The Woodlands began with a multiyear contract in October, 1974, by which the 160-member Association of Tennis Professionals agreed to make its home in the new town. One month later, soon after The Woodlands opened in October, the Northwest Rotary Club Tennis Tournament staged its first annual competition on the new town's ten outdoor courts. In 1976 two major tournaments came to The Woodlands, the Italian National Doubles Tennis Championship and the U.S. Professional Doubles Championship. Equally prestigious events soon followed, including the nationally televised World Tennis Tour Mixed Doubles Classic, starring world-class competitors like Martina Navratilova, Marty Riessen, Billie Jean King, Sandy Mayer, Rod Laver, Kerry Melville Reid, Rosie Casals, and Charles Pasarell.[14]

Although successful in many ways, by the late 1970s the meshing of environment and recreational amenities and eye-catching sports events had fallen short of attaining the commercial-industrial and socioeconomic mixes desired for the new town. Thus during 1977 The Woodlands Development Corporation embarked on two special program

13. *Conroe Daily Courier,* October 18, 1974, August 8, 1976; *Woodlands Sun,* October 30, 1974; *Houston Post,* November 16, 1975, January 25, 1976; The Woodlands Development Corporation, news releases, April 12, July 19, July 20, August 9, 1977, July 26, September 11, 1979.

14. *Conroe Daily Courier,* October 28, 1974; *Houston Post,* October 28, 1974; The Woodlands Development Corporation, news release, April 6, 1977. Additional sports events staged in The Woodlands included professional boxing, running marathons, wrestling matches, and ice-skating competitions.

designed to provide a more satisfactory mix of low- and moderate-income housing. One program, developed with the aid and approval of HUD, required the developer to offer 824 home lots at prices low enough to enable builders to sell homes in the $29,000–$49,500 range during 1978, plus an additional 455 lots for homes ranging from $42,000 to $54,000 in 1979. A second program, also agreed to by HUD, provided that The Woodlands Development Corporation would make enough land available to apartment-complex developers at or below market value to accommodate up to 420 federally assisted rental units. Subsequently Landmark Properties, Inc., of Dallas, completed negotiations with The Woodlands Development Corporation for the purchase of a site for a 120-unit, rent-assisted apartment complex, and the National Corporation for Housing Partnerships of Washington, D.C., agreed to an option for construction of a rent-assisted complex of 275 to 300 units for senior citizens.[15]

Pending initiation of these socially oriented projects, overall development activity during 1977 continued apace. In February construction began on the first phase of Grogan's Landing Apartments, a $3.6 million complex planned ultimately to contain 400 units; work continued on a second eighteen-hole golf course; sale of residential and commercial lots began in the second village, Panther Creek; land clearing, utilizing an innovative "open burning" system, began in the Technology Park; groundbreaking ceremonies launched the construction of the third and fourth office buildings in the Office Park; the Jack Eckerd Corporation's warehouse and distribution center in the Trade Center neared completion; and 38 townhouses in the Settler's Corner neighborhood of Grogan's Mill Village approached completion as construction began on an additional 38 units, concluding the four-phase townhouse neighborhood development with a total of 150 homes.[16]

Under the new leadership of Edward P. Lee, who took over as president in November, 1977, The Woodlands Development Corporation continued general development during 1978 but with a shift in emphasis. "We will stress," Lee announced early in the year, "sales and

15. James F. Dausch to Robinson G. Lapp, n.d., WDC Papers; *Woodlands Sun,* October 27, 1976; *Woodlands Villager,* December 7, 1977; The Woodlands Development Corporation, news release, May 10, 1977; Mitchell Energy and Development Corporation, Annual Report, Year Ended January 31, 1977, p. 22; Annual Report, Year Ended January 31, 1978, p. 25.

16. The Woodlands Development Corporation, news releases, February 9, February 23, March 24, November 10, June 9, October 25, November 16, December 11, December 20, 1977; Mitchell Energy and Development Corporation, Annual Report, Year Ended January 31, 1978, pp. 23, 25.

leases for commercial and industrial properties" and concurrently announced the opening of a 300-acre Technology Park for companies
that wished to establish research-and-development facilities in a "think-
tank atmosphere." Soon thereafter The Woodlands Development Corporation completed negotiations for residential land sales valued at $3.8
million, and construction began on the first sixteen units of Landmark
Properties' rent-assisted Fawnridge Apartments. Theodore Nelson, director of builder land sales for The Woodlands Development Corporation, pointed out that the lots would be used solely to build homes
in the $38,000–$60,000 range. "The majority of homes in The Woodlands," Nelson added, "sold for under $60,000 over the last four years.
The Woodlands is committed to offering homes which are affordable
to people with varying incomes. We want all people to be able to make
The Woodlands their hometown."

In late July, George Mitchell announced plans for a 350,000-square-
foot building costing more than $13 million in the Office Park to house
Mitchell Energy and Development Corporation. The building would
consist of three connected six-story units containing large exterior areas
of tinted glass and trapezoid-shaped floor designs. He intended, Mitchell added, that the headquarters building would be "the keystone for
an important new commercial development stage at The Woodlands."
Also, in late 1978 the first supermarket opened in the new town, and,
in the largest nonrail-served commercial-industrial land sale in the history of The Woodlands to that point, Betz Process Chemicals, Inc., purchased a 19.1-acre site in the Metro Center. Almost simultaneously
Kirsch/Clark Properties, Inc., announced a joint-venture agreement for
the development of Grogan's Square I, a 12,000-square-foot shopping
center on a 1.1-acre tract in Grogan's Mill Village.

George Mitchell, however, sounded a less happy note as 1978
drew to a close with the announcement of a postponement in the construction of his company's office headquarters, plus a significant reduction in costs, because of rising interest rates and budgetary restraints
necessary to ensure future financial health.[17]

Record revenues achieved by Mitchell Energy and Development
Corporation during 1979, however, prompted Mitchell to observe that
"relocation of the commercial, industrial and recreational centers of
the United States continues to tilt in our direction, and the long-term
soundness of investment in Houston area real estate becomes more
evident." Moreover, he reported, "in a two-year period, our real estate

17. *Woodlands Villager,* March 8, May 24, July 26, September 27, November 29,
1978; The Woodlands Development Corporation, news release, September 21, 1978.   **111**

operations have progressed from a $2.8 million operating loss to an $8.7 million operating profit." Newfound prosperity combined with indicators of continuing financial viability to trigger a spate of activity in all developmental components in the new town throughout 1979. Between February and the end of April, The Woodlands Development Corporation began construction of a two-building, 102,600-square-foot warehouse and distribution center in the Trade Center; accepted final bids for the construction of phase 1 of Creekwood Neighborhood Park, in Panther Creek Village; commenced work on two buildings totaling 61,200 square feet in the Technology Park, and began construction of a 24,450-square-foot addition to The Wharf shopping mall in Grogan's Mill Village. In August construction began on the previously postponed Mitchell Energy and Development Corporation headquarters with its original budget virtually intact, and in September, in a transaction described as "the largest lease signed to date in The Woodlands," the Western Division of Superior Oil Company, then the nation's largest independent oil-and-gas company, leased a five-story building under construction in the Office Park.

Less spectacular but equally important events combined with the foregoing to make 1979 a banner year for the new town: the launching of a "speculative" building program by Ryland Homes because of the company's "faith in the continued growth and viability of the new home market"; the start of a $6.5 million 268-unit apartment complex on a thirteen-acre site in Grogan's Mill Village; the opening of Tamarac Pines Apartments, the first rent-assisted project in The Woodlands for the elderly and handicapped; the purchase of tracts in the Trade Center and the Metro Center by APS-Materials, Inc., and Snap-on Tools Corporation; and record high new home sales, 65 percent of which, for the first time since the 1974 opening, were purchases by buyers outside the greater Houston area.[18]

The pace of development achieved during 1979 accelerated in the following year. By spring construction involving over one million square feet of office, industrial, and retail space, either planned or under way, led R. Douglas Leonhard, senior vice-president of commercial and industrial development, to observe, "It is the most commercial and industrial space under construction at one time in the history of The Woodlands." Major building activity included the first commercial de-

18. Mitchell Energy and Development Corporation, Annual Report, Year Ended January 31, 1979, pp. 4–5; Woodlands Villager, January 17, March 14, March 21, May 16, August 1, September 19, October 21, November 7, December 12, December 19, 1979; The Woodlands Development Corporation, news releases, April 3, October 3, December 5, 1979.

velopment in Panther Creek Village, office buildings to house Superior Oil and Mitchell Energy and Development Corporation, a 214,500-square-foot addition to The Wharf shopping mall, and 102,000 square feet of warehouse and distribution facilities in the Trade Center.

Increased commercial-industrial development and continued vigorous new-home sales and apartment leases resulted, of course, in population and employment growth. By midsummer, 1980, the population had reached 8,818, the number of employers had grown to 170, and the total of nonconstruction permanent employees had swelled to 3,350. These advances, plus record-breaking new-homes sales during June, led Roger Galatas, vice-president of residential development, to predict a yearly increase of 1,000 employment opportunities in the new town over the next biennium. The decision of Petroscience Corporation in early August to relocate its headquarters in a $3 million, three-story office building next to the West Golf Course provided further reason for optimism about future growth. Petroscience chose The Woodlands, the company's president announced, "not only because of its proximity to the dynamic Houston business center, but also because of the planned potential growth of the area."[19]

These significant events paled in comparison to the stimulus provided by Mitchell Energy and Development Corporation's move, including almost 350 employees, into its newly completed office building on November 1, 1980. Appropriately enough, the relocation of the parent company's headquarters nearly coincided with the arrival in The Woodlands of the Mike and Mary Levy family—an event which elevated the new town's population to a milestone 10,000. As the new year approached, total investment in The Woodlands reached approximately $192 million. About 10,000 residents lived in over 4,000 homes, townhouses, or apartments, and a force of 4,000 worked for nearly 200 employers.[20]

Calendar year 1981 proved to be an even more successful, record-breaking period for The Woodlands. Although the nationwide economic recession dropped national housing starts to the lowest total in thirty-five years, builders in The Woodlands added 1,290 new residential dwellings—860 houses and 430 apartments—a 25 percent increase over the number added in 1980. Galatas attributed this performance to the lure provided to businesses by the environmental and aesthetic advantages of the new town. The location, or relocation, of those enterprises

19. *Woodlands Villager,* April 9, April 16, June 11, July 16, August 6, 1980; "Fact Sheet: The Woodlands New Town," WDC Papers.

20. *Woodlands Villager,* November 6, 1980; The Woodlands Development Corporation, news release, December 31, 1980.

Residential area in The Woodlands.

brought well-paid professional and white-collar employees eager to live and work in The Woodlands. During the year 280 employers leased over 3 million square feet of commercial and industrial space and employed almost 5,000 workers—an increase of nearly 800 employees over the previous twelve-month period.[21]

Moreover, during the year management intensified its efforts to continue the particular attraction The Woodlands, with its wooded, campuslike environment, held for technical, scientific, and academic organizations. A donation of a 100-acre site led to the organization of the Houston Area Research Center, a consortium of the University of Texas, Rice University, Texas A&M University, and the University of Houston

21. The Woodlands Development Corporation, news releases, May 21, September 9, September 18, October 16, 1981, February 4, 1982.

A typical neighborhood in The Woodlands.

which ultimately employed several hundred scientists, academicians, and administrators. Also, Pennzoil acquired a 40-acre site on which to establish a technology center funded by an initial investment of $30 million, and negotiations neared completion with the Texas Medical Center, Inc., representing thirty Houston hospital and medical-research institutions, to accept a donation of 150 acres of land for the establishment of a major research facility.[22]

A year of confident expansion ended as it started. In December, J. Leonard Rogers announced plans for the construction of a twelve-story hotel in The Woodlands. The company's decision to embark on yet another major commercial investment, with construction slated to

22. Mitchell Energy and Development Corporation, Annual Report, Year Ended January 31, 1982, p. 25.

Aerial view, East Golf Course.

begin in late 1982, arose, Rogers said, out of the "continuing growth of Montgomery County and the demand for additional hotels and meeting spaces." When completed, the facility would be "the largest, single-structure hotel in Montgomery County."[23]

Inspired by the successes of the immediately preceding years, officials of The Woodlands Development Corporation made enthusiastic predictions about even greater growth in 1982, particularly in the development of commercial and industrial properties. In January, 1982,

23. The Woodlands Development Corporation, news release, December 17, 1981. The company subsequently suspended plans for building the hotel as the full impact of economic recession settled on the Houston area. The proliferation of high-rise hotels in the Intercontinental Airport area further softened demand. Interview with J. Leonard Rogers, October 31, 1984.

Headquarters office, Mitchell Energy and Development Corporation, The Woodlands.

R. Douglas Leonhard publicly reviewed plans for new projects during the coming year and ongoing construction on earlier starts totaling 650,000 square feet. Planned new starts included four office buildings in the Metro Center and retail-store construction in Panther Creek Village Square. Development begun in 1981 and scheduled for completion in 1982 included three office and professional buildings (The Woodlands Professional Building, the Woodstead Office Building, and Pine Circle Technology Center) in the Metro Center. The magnitude of these developments lessened, however, with the announcement by The Woodlands Development Corporation in March, 1982, of a joint-venture agreement with Homart Development Company, a subsidiary of Sears, Roebuck and Company, to undertake construction of a 75.7-acre shopping mall

117

near the Metro Center. Targeted for construction in the late 1980s, the mall would contain over a million square feet of shopping space.[24]

While the proposed shopping mall augured well for the future, the beginning during 1982 of phase 1 construction in Cochran's Crossing Village marked an immediate milestone. The third of six proposed villages, Cochran's Crossing was to be the largest in both land area and population. In addition to residential construction, phase 1 involved creation of a major flood-control and drainage system capped by Bear Branch Reservoir, just north of the village. Construction of the reservoir, contracted by the Houston engineering firm Brown and Root, entailed a 2,400-foot earthen dam containing a 400-foot concrete spillway. The completed dam would form a 70-acre reservoir or lake with an average depth of 18 feet, capable of supporting fish and other wildlife. In addition to its more practical and recreational functions, the $2 million reservoir would, according to Plato Pappas, vice-president of land development, provide a "visual amenity."[25]

As in previous years, brisk construction activity and publicity given to planned development stimulated residential home sales. Indeed, 1982 marked another record year as sales reached 1,011 – an increase of 15 percent over the previous year's record – and by year's end population had reached 16,000, with some 260 employers employing over 5,000 workers.[26]

From the start of construction activity in the new town The Woodlands Development Corporation exercised utmost care to preserve the natural environment. Thus most home-builder contracts stipulated a number of safeguards designed to minimize destructive practices on building tracts. Furthermore, the corporation practiced what it preached – its staff at all times included environmental planners and engineers charged with the responsibility of implementing the project's development plan. The corporation also appointed Bill Kendrick field superintendent of environmental control. In 1972, Kendrick had participated in a U.S. Soil Conservation Service survey of soil types in The Woodlands, and upon completion of the survey in 1974 he had left government employment to join the staff of the new town.

A zealot in the performance of his duties, Kendrick, in addition to his other responsibilities, inspected every tract to be cleared before concrete was poured. "If moving a driveway four feet will allow us to

24. The Woodlands Development Corporation, news releases, January 1, March 4, 1982; Mitchell Energy and Development Corporation, Annual Report, Year Ended January 31, 1983, p. 20.

25. The Woodlands Development Corporation, news release, February 19, 1983.

26. Ibid., July 16, September 11, September 23, 1982.

Excavation of Lake Woodlands, 1985.

save a dogwood tree," Kendrick asserted, "I see that the driveway is moved." Construction-site preparation often included uprooting of trees up to fifteen feet tall by hydraulic spade for transplanting, plus installation of streets and other paved areas before the erection of buildings. In large cleared areas, such as golf courses, where inevitable damage to root systems occurred, the corporation conducted extensive reforestation programs, planting up to fifteen thousand elm, cottonwood, oak, cedar, mulberry, and pine seedlings. According to Carlton Gipson, this planting program would "give Mother Nature a five year head start."[27]

To enhance the natural environment further, The Woodlands De-

27. Ibid., February 9, February 23, April 21, 1977. The builder of Village Square Apartments described the complex as "one of the finest projects I've ever done" and **119**

Lake Woodlands, 1986.

velopment Corporation also set aside a three-acre sanctuary containing an especially wide variety of native vegetation and in January, 1978, inaugurated an annual "Arbor Day–Tree Rush" weekend. During each celebration the company distributed to residents thousands of seedlings for landscaping. On the eve of the third Arbor Day weekend Bill Kendrick announced: "Our goal is to have each family take home 10 seedlings. We are dedicated to enhancing the natural forests of this area, and we are inviting the residents to take an active part." In November, 1978, the same concern prompted George Mitchell to express his deepening dismay over cutting practices being pursued by

added, "I was asked to save as many trees and vegetation as possible . . . making it awkward to get construction materials and equipment to the site. But the end result was well worth the extra effort." Ibid., July 31, 1980.

a rival developer in southern Montgomery County. "We should be cautious," he counseled his colleagues, "not to do the same thing." Mitchell reported that he had met with an officer of the offending company who had agreed to a cooperative program to preserve the forests. Mitchell warned, however: "In my opinion, in the last two years, Southern Montgomery County has deteriorated to a large extent. If we do not do something to remedy this, it will reach disaster proportions in another five years."[28]

Despite the most careful planning and the best intentions, however, development inevitably left wounds, and those wounds deepened as the pace of construction increased, as did the numbers of residents and their varying awareness of environmental concerns. Hence during the virtual construction moratorium of 1975 little or no criticism of the developer's environmental practices emanated from residential ranks. Heightened construction from 1976 through 1979 likewise elicited few complaints, with the lone exception of charges by a resident member of the Woodlands Community Association that utility contractors in The Woodlands unnecessarily wreaked havoc with the environment. The board of directors responded by approving a mild resolution admonishing contractors to minimize damage. Peak development during the early 1980s brought with it the first discordant notes from residents, who typically ranked the natural environment as the new town's major asset. Some homeowners reacted stridently in November, 1981, to The Woodlands Development Corporation's approval of construction of a service station on Grogan's Mill Road. Most of the disturbed householders argued that the service station's location and design violated the project development plan. One couple correctly pointed out that all residences in The Woodlands received constant scrutiny by the Residential Design Review Committee to ensure conformity to the natural environment. "We respect this policy," they added, "and believe that it should apply to all commercial development as well." The issue culminated in a compromise—the oil company agreed to alterations designed to blend the facility into the landscape, and the residents, some of them grudgingly, accepted the environmentally more harmonious design and the convenience of consumer service near at hand.[29]

In much the same vein, and certainly in more compelling fashion, a group of twenty-three students at Knox Junior High School voiced

28. Ibid., January 4, January 10, 1978; *Woodlands Villager,* January 16, 1980; George Mitchell to Morris Thompson, Ed Dreiss, and Max Newland, November 14, 1978, WDC Papers.

29. *Woodlands Villager,* July 13, 1977, November 11, 1981.

their concern, whether their own or partly inspired by parents and teachers, over the rapid pace of development. The youngsters wrote:

> We moved to The Woodlands to live in the trees, and now many are being destroyed so that buildings can be constructed. We understand that The Woodlands must build in order to survive, but we do think there should be limitations. . . . All the homes in The Woodlands used to be surrounded by many trees. Now there are only a few, if any at all. . . . Many businessmen are being selfish now by destroying the beauty that will be ours tomorrow. We appreciate the efforts that The Woodlands is putting out to keep the looks of the buildings . . . natural, but nothing can replace the beauty that was cut down. . . . It's called The Woodlands, but we are losing our woods.

Randall L. Woods, vice-president of public relations for the corporation, assured the students that the developer shared their desire to keep The Woodlands beautiful and pointed out that the need to rectify a serious drainage problem had dictated at least part of the most damaging development. Nonetheless, Woods concluded, "through seven years of solid growth, The Woodlands has been developed with a vision for the future and we want to assure you that we intend to do everything we can to make The Woodlands a special place for you."[30]

Proper drainage, as Woods and many others contended, did pose special problems in the new town — problems sometimes beyond the developer's control, but usually correctable given time for implementation of development plans. In completing and perfecting the new town's drainage system, the corporation occasionally found itself in an unwanted adversary relationship with residents of neighboring subdivisions and with some homeowners in The Woodlands.

Following resolution of drainage-system disputes between The Woodlands Development Corporation and the developer, residents, and Oak Ridge North MUD in 1974, harmonious relations prevailed until the summer of 1976. In late August the corporation began clearing a 150-foot-wide strip in preparation for a drainage ditch on The Woodlands property just north of Oak Ridge North Drive. Residents in the area welcomed construction of the ditch because its north-south course would divert water that was flowing west to east across their property. A furor developed, however, when homeowners learned that the cleared strip would begin 10 feet from their backyard fences. One resident protested: "We're not against the ditch, we just want them to leave some of our lovely trees. I always thought that Mr. Mitchell was for environment and habitat, now he's coming right up to our back-

30. Ibid., December 18, 1981.

yards and cutting all our trees." A nonplused Plato Pappas professed incredulity at the residents' wrath and wryly commented, "I gave them ten feet and now they want more." The homeowners steadfastly argued that a 50-foot belt had been promised and refused to accept less until Jimmie Edwards, a state representative, intervened to arrange a compromise providing for a 20-foot belt.[31]

Two years later flood-plagued homeowners in Timberlake and Timber Ridge subdivisions adjacent to The Woodlands and at a lower ground elevation than that of the new town petitioned Montgomery County Commissioners' Court for aid. In addition to requesting an investigation of the new town's planned drainage system, the petitioners charged that their flood woes resulted from runoff caused by construction in the new town and expressed their fear that contemplated ditches to drain some 350 acres in The Woodlands would overload already flood-prone Spring Creek, further endangering their homes. Vernon P. Robbins, senior vice-president of engineering and land development for The Woodlands Development Corporation, responded that engineering studies indicated the proposed ditches would raise the water level of Spring Creek by only half an inch over the next 100 years. He also pointed out that water currently drained into Spring Creek by way of a swale and the ditches would therefore "just be more formalized and stop any sheet damage." The engineers' report and Robbins's appraisal of them proved correct; completion of the drainage system ultimately minimized flooding in the two subdivisions.[32]

In The Woodlands the natural drainage system, augmented by ditches, channels, berms, and retention lakes, sufficed to prevent flooding under normal conditions. It is also true that early in the planning process Mitchell and his consultants agreed to restrict all home construction to areas above the 100-year floodplain. "I hope," Mitchell announced, "we can lead the way and other developers will have to do the same." Torrential rains which often beset the Texas Gulf Coast, plus the generally flat terrain in The Woodlands, nonetheless proved at times to be too much despite all precautions. Uncommonly heavy rains flooded a few homes in the lowest-lying areas before the drainage system was completed. Homeowners in such areas, understandably dismayed by a few inches of water in their homes, expressed frustration and worse—especially if their appeals to the corporation went unanswered or promised completion of drainage systems failed to meet

31. *Conroe Daily Courier,* August 30, September 1, 1976. J. Leonard Rogers pointed out that actually the compromise created a thirty-three-foot belt between the ditch and the houses because of the need for a thirteen-to-fifteen-foot working area.

32. *Woodlands Villager,* August 23, September 6, September 13, 1978.

Plato Pappas (left) and Vernon Robbins inspecting a drainage-ditch site.

projected timetables.[33] Other residents, beleaguered by water standing in their yards or streets, sometimes found the time lapse between complaint and remedy inexplicable, while still others found cause for righteous indignation over what they considered precipitous and irresponsible response. In one instance a drainage ditch serving a cluster of homes in Panther Creek Village, clogged either by negligence or by homeowners' attempts to disguise its existence or simply inadequate for its purpose, failed to carry off standing water. To the dismay of the residents MUD engineers arrived without prior warning and proceeded to widen and deepen the ditch by twelve to eighteen inches. In the process they stripped lawn sod and left an exposed, unsightly gully.

33. *Houston Post,* August 26, 1973; *Woodlands Villager,* April 25, 1979, July 2, 1980.

Incensed by the disfiguring of their landscapes, the residents denounced the work as a "quick fix." One of their number, heedless of the developer's lack of responsibility for MUD's actions, went further and castigated the corporation's development design as an unqualified error. "Why should we," the irate householder asked, "have to pay for their mistakes?"[34]

This incident, although trivial and atypical of conditions in The Woodlands, assumes greater importance when viewed as part of the complex and often confounding aspects of building a new town. During one of their first encounters in 1969, Richard P. Browne, when asked by George Mitchell what it took to build a new town, responded with a list of eleven requirements, all of a rather obvious and practical nature. When Mitchell questioned the completeness of the list, Browne added a twelfth and, in his opinion, the most vital prerequisite. A successful developer must be a cultural anthropologist, Browne advised Mitchell, because "the lives of very real people are at stake and if one has the audacity to claim the right to build a city, one has to face the obligations inherent in such a monumental undertaking. A community is much more than sticks and bricks."[35]

34. *Woodlands Villager,* July 2, 1980.
35. Ibid., October 14, 1981.

8. A New Town's Social Goals

THE HUMAN FACTOR

Both the New Communities Act of 1968 and the Urban Growth and New Community Development Act of 1970 stressed the social values to be gained by new-town development. The 1970 legislation, for example, stated that among other purposes the law was intended to "encourage and support development which will assure our communities of adequate tax bases, community services, job opportunities, and well-balanced neighborhoods in socially, economically, and physically attractive living environments."[1]

In keeping with congressional objectives, The Woodlands Development Plan included provision for a Design Review Committee, composed mainly of qualified professionals but also including some residents, with "absolute right to approve or disapprove any and all proposed site plans and structures" in the project. The committee was also empowered to "review and approve all graphics . . . including design of billboards, traffic signs, and of all signs for commercial and office buildings, and industrial, institutional, and cultural facilities." The plan additionally provided that the developer would use his "best efforts" to establish a comprehensive health-care program, including preventive as well as standard systems. In a catchall section entitled "Innovation," the developer pledged himself to employ advanced techniques in design and technology and to provide community facilities and services, communication, security and transit systems, collection of data for

126   1. *U.S. Statutes at Large*, 84:1791.

management decisions, and cultural activities. Finally, the plan ensured resident participation in governance by the formation of quasi-government organizations and community associations. This section also required the developer to establish communications with the residents through orientation meetings, planning discussions, publication of a monthly newsletter, and biannual briefing meetings covering general development plans. Resident suggestions would be incorporated into the development plan "where feasible."[2]

During the early years of development The Woodlands Development Corporation failed to attain a number of those innovative social goals, with the significant exception of environmental design. The reasons for failure—absence of corporate will, defective management decisions, lack of funds, heavy construction costs, the economic recession, or a mixture thereof—are debatable. Donald R. Gebert, executive director of Interfaith and a friendly critic of The Woodlands Development Corporation, considers George Mitchell "an absolute visionary" who anticipated the difficulties which would inevitably arise out of conflicting social goals and attempted to minimize friction by establishing a department of institutional planning. "And that is why," Gebert asserts, "he asked the religious bodies to come together and form their own corporation. The plan was that . . . Interfaith would be a liaison with that department . . . and that Interfaith would really have the pulse of the community." The financial crunch of 1974–75, however, forced abandonment of social planning in what Gebert considers the "most significant human event that happened in The Woodlands [and] the one least noticed."[3]

Charles Kelly, head of the institutional planning department, which was eliminated early in 1975 and never replaced, sees lack of company commitment as the primary reason for the failure to establish social services. "They [the developers] were," he argues, "looking to somebody else to do that. One of the main sources, they hoped, would be the churches, who would develop a social-services program that would benefit the community."[4] If Mitchell and The Woodlands Development Corporation really did expect the churches to fulfill that function, successful handling of church-related matters demanded ceaseless coop-

2. Development Plan, exhibits G26, G31–G46. The covenants of the Woodlands Community Association changed the name of the Design Review Committee to the Development Standards Committee and provided for the election of a Residential Design Review Committee in each village. Articles of Incorporation of The Woodlands Community Association, WDC Papers.
3. Interview with Donald R. Gebert, September 30, 1982.
4. Interview with Charles Kelly, August 31, 1982.

erative effort and open communications, neither of which completely escaped the cataclysmic events of 1975–77.

As previously noted, from the outset of the project Mitchell sought to include the religious community in the planning process. For that purpose he invited leaders of several denominations to a series of meetings, which resulted in the formation of the Religious Institutional Planning Committee. In a statement of goals, "Towards an Interfaith Covenant," adopted on February 10, 1972, the committee leaders affirmed their mutual respect for denominational integrity and principles but agreed to "share facilities and ministries in understanding and mutual respect for the particular worship expressions of our particular groups." On October 5, 1973, to provide coherent leadership as the new town progressed beyond the planning stage to actual construction, the group organized itself as The Woodlands Religious Community, Inc. (WRC).[5]

Almost immediately a serious and never totally reconciled difference of opinion developed between Mitchell and the WRC. Mitchell remained steadfastly committed to the Columbia interfaith system, in which denominations shared facilities built before the congregations were formed. The buildings were to be paid for through percentage assessments levied on each user. The WRC, on the other hand, came to believe, particularly after some of its board members visited Columbia, that the system caused alienation of church members, poor church attendance, and a decline in revenues which forced denominations to tap mission funds to pay assessments. The WRC believed that these "tragic results" could be avoided.

Another point of disagreement involved responsibility for the provision of child day-care facilities. Mitchell believed that the religious community should provide such services. WRC, however, in a decision slowly arrived at and predicated on the Columbia example, saw its role as a guiding organization which led but did not become involved in day-to-day implementation of programs, including the provision of facilities for any purpose.[6]

Although avoiding direct participation as a builder of facilities, the WRC, because of its perceived role as a facilitator of human-service programs and as a liaison between denominations and the developer, continued to be intimately involved with Mitchell and The Woodlands Development Corporation. That relationship also became strained from

5. Alvin H. Franzmeier and Donald R. Gebert, *The Woodlands Experience: An Unfinished History of the Interfaith Movement in a New Town in Texas*, pp. 2, 7.
6. Ibid., p. 11.

time to time because of communications lapses which necessitated a number of formalized agreements.

The first such compact grew out of The Woodlands Development Corporation's independent negotiations during March, 1974, with Lord of Life Lutheran Church for purchase of its property, situated directly east of I-45. The corporation needed the land for construction of a second overpass and proposed that in the event of a sale the church relocate in The Woodlands near the proposed Tamina Mill Community Center. When the WRC learned of the proposal, which it considered a breach of the spirit if not the letter of its verbal agreement with Mitchell that the WRC would be a party to negotiations involving religious groups, the WRC asked The Woodlands Development Corporation to agree to a formal letter of understanding. The letter, agreed to by The Woodlands Development Corporation on April 1, 1974, and later confirmed by Mitchell, defined the respective responsibilities and obligations of the two organizations. The company acknowledged the WRC's responsibility for planning and implementation of religious-community development and as negotiator for The Woodlands Development Corporation with congregations and judicatories contemplating entry into The Woodlands. The corporation also committed itself to provide the WRC with continuous access to its land-use planning department, marketing group, and top management to keep the WRC constantly informed of policy decisions. The company also agreed to refer all communications from religious groups to the WRC as the recognized negotiating body. Unfortunately, officers of The Woodlands Development Corporation subsequently failed to honor the commitment to keep the WRC informed of policy decisions.[7]

Rising land prices in The Woodlands, caused in part by rising development costs, provided yet another source of tension in an already troubled relationship. Early population-growth projections by corporation officers—four hundred people by early 1974, two thousand by the end of the year, and seven thousand five hundred by the end of 1975—far exceeded actual figures. The inflated estimates stimulated pressure for speedy construction of worship facilities.[8] During the spring of 1973, The Woodlands Development Corporation offered the WRC a 5-acre tract in the Sawmill Community Center at a cost ranging from $10,000 to $12,000 an acre, a figure close to the company's cost. In July, 1973, the WRC allocated $1,281 for planning purposes on the tract, but in September, 1973, the organization formally renounced the role of

7. Ibid., p. 30.
8. Ibid., p. 8.

builder of human-service facilities. In December, 1973, Charles Kelly informed the WRC that the original offer had been changed to 2.69 acres at $12,000 an acre and asked that the purchase be completed by January 10, 1974. In the interim population projections had risen even higher—one thousand seven hundred families by the end of 1974 and three thousand eight hundred within eighteen months—and in January, 1974, the WRC signed a purchase contract for 1.847 acres in the Sawmill Community Center at $12,000 an acre.[9]

Following this initial land purchase additional transactions during 1974 and 1975 by individual denominations, with the WRC (now known as Interfaith) acting as negotiator, were made without a definitive statement by The Woodlands Development Corporation of its land policy. In July, 1976, Robinson G. Lapp, the company's director of community operations, enunciated the corporation's policy. In most instances, Lapp stated, the company envisioned church parks of one to three acres, priced approximately at cost—$13,000 to $16,000 an acre—over the next two years. Churches choosing to purchase single sites would pay prices closer to existing commercial rates. "We are committed," Lapp informed Interfaith, "to working through the WRC and making land available to religious bodies at a reduced price. For this reason, we are also quite interested in the WRC's commitment to the church park concept as a means of reducing land usage and encouraging cooperation among the groups. It is our policy to justify the lower prices on the basis of demonstrated land savings." On the other hand, Lapp added, the corporation's generosity would not extend to congregations unwilling to conform to the church-park model: "Where religious bodies do not wish to cooperate with each other, or to place their institutions in spots where some sharing of parking and/or other spaces or programs is feasible, we simply shall not be able to provide land at other than commercial prices."[10] Although this decision was economically sound, the exclusion of uncooperative denominations certainly did little to reverse The Woodlands Development Corporation's image among some residents and outsiders as an uncompromising, unresponsive corporate entity concerned solely with profit.

Subsequent company actions did little to alter the image. Despite Lapp's consistent advocacy of his stated policy, some corporate officers either did not understand the commitment or were unaware of its existence. Consequently, over a two-year period lands offered as church sites doubled and tripled in price, to $30,000 and $54,450 an

9. Ibid., pp. 13–14.
10. Ibid., pp. 36–38.

acre. Interfaith's objections and pleas for consultations went unheeded until April, 1978, when G. W. Kirsch, director of commercial sales and leasing, formally confirmed a shift away from Lapp's pricing policy. Kirsch wrote: "For those judicatories selecting sites which fit the church [park] concept, land will be priced . . . at fair market value less 25%. Those bodies which must select sites other than church campus locations would pay fair market value. Under this policy, it will, of course, not be possible to price sites in advance of their selection by a particular body, as fair market value will be a constantly changing thing."[11]

The price uncertainties in this new policy threatened the survival of Interfaith, since its financial support was based largely on the service it provided denominations by negotiating reduced land prices. Discussions between representatives of Interfaith and the corporation became increasingly intense until the issue was partly resolved, with the aid of Robinson G. Lapp, on July 31, 1978. On that date Edward P. Lee, president of The Woodlands Development Corporation, committed the company to sell all church sites at $29,000 an acre during the remainder of 1978. The new policy included a 10 percent price escalation in 1979, and the company agreed to give Interfaith four months' notice of any future price increases.[12]

This agreement provided a more satisfactory working arrangement between the company and Interfaith but left unresolved the question of who was to provide the necessary human services in The Woodlands. That question and the increasing concern of some residents that they had no substantive voice in governance contributed significantly to what Donald R. Gebert has styled "New Town Syndrome." This phenomenon, in many ways similar to the malaise suffered by inhabitants of nineteenth-century company towns, includes the frustrations, alienation, and apathy often demonstrated by new-town residents. The symptoms develop out of unrealistic expectations of utopia, the loneliness of transplantation, the rapidity of change, and the sense of lack of ownership.[13]

Gebert, an ordained Lutheran minister and the first executive director of Interfaith, assumed that position on May 1, 1975. He had previously served as a missionary in Guyana, as an urban pastor in Philadelphia's inner city, and as a community organizer with the Philadelphia Foundation, a well-endowed philanthropic organization. A self-styled crusader at heart whose "real interest has always been with the

11. Ibid., pp. 38–40.
12. Ibid., p. 41.
13. Ibid., pp. 42–45; interview with Donald R. Gebert, September 30, 1982.   **131**

have nots and trying to get the have nots mobilized . . . to get themselves into the mainstream of what was happening in society," Gebert plunged into his new role with a zeal that continued undiminished until his resignation in late 1984.[14]

"When I came down here," he recalls, "all of that experience was a perfect credential because what you have here is an entirely transplanted population into a new town context." To Gebert the nature of the population and the absence of traditional institutions meant that the success of the new town hinged on "people working with each other creating their own institutions, creating their own ways of getting themselves together."[15] Joined by a small group of like-minded activist residents, Gebert devoted his efforts to finding ways to motivate residents to form a community of people, not just houses.

To counteract the residents' apathy, stemming largely from their perception of total corporate ownership and their lack of control over their destinies, Gebert and his associates first sought resident participation in The Woodlands Community Association. As originally planned and established by The Woodlands Development Corporation, the association was intended to function in two major ways. First, it was to serve as a nonprofit municipal corporation which owned and maintained amenities in The Woodlands and provided city services like garbage collection, fire protection, and mosquito control. In this role the association would be eligible to receive federal grants for recreational and open-space improvements. Second, the association would provide residents with a voice in their governance.

The Woodlands Development Corporation, like all other developers of new towns, considered it absolutely essential that the company have majority control of the community association during most of the development period to ensure compliance with its design plan.[16] For that reason the association's covenants included a complicated formula for resident representation on the board of directors. The covenants established a nine-member board of directors, eight appointed by The Woodlands Development Corporation and one elected by the residents. The total board membership would eventually expand to fifteen. Resident-elected members would increase with the number of completed residential units until the total dwellings reached 39,000. At that time residents would elect eight members, and the company would

14. Interview with Donald R. Gebert, September 30, 1982; Franzmeier and Gebert, *Woodlands Experience,* pp. 23–24.

15. Interview with Donald R. Gebert, September 30, 1982.

16. "Woodlands Village Chronicle" (manuscript in WDC Papers), November 29, 1972.

appoint seven. This procedure would continue until 1992, when total control would pass to the residents.[17]

As construction on the project lagged far behind projections, The Woodlands Development Corporation voluntarily surrendered to the residents one of its appointive positions on the association's board of directors. It also acquiesced to resident election of a third member before the required number of dwellings had been built. The corporation's generosity did not, however, nullify its seven-to-three majority or the likelihood of conflict inherent in the system. Joel Deretchin, who replaced Robinson G. Lapp as director of community operations and president of the community association in May, 1981, aptly described the volatile situation he inherited and at the same time underscored the corporation's characteristic willingness to accommodate the residents' aspirations as long as the integrity of the design plan remained intact. "We all grow up," Deretchin observed, "believing in democratic institutions with elected representatives. People move into The Woodlands and find that the most governmental-like thing we have going is the community association and lo and behold the developer appoints the majority of the members of the board of directors. That is foreign to our way of thinking as Americans."[18]

Two months after Gebert's arrival in late April, 1975, he met with a small group of "concerned" residents, who established the Grogan's Mill Village Association. In October, 1975, the association received permission from The Woodlands Development Corporation to elect its first resident representative to the community association's board of directors.[19] The same group of residents, led by Gebert and Jack O'Sullivan, also began publishing the first independent community newsletter. Originally called the *Grogan's Mill Villager,* edited by O'Sullivan, produced in mimeographed form, and hand-delivered by Gebert and his wife, the newsletter gradually grew into the *Woodlands Villager,* a multipage newspaper with a weekly press run of five thousand copies by mid-1977 and twenty-three thousand by the fall of 1982.[20]

Formation of the village association and publication of a community newspaper established avenues of communication for residents and forums for at least an advisory role in company policy decisions. They did not, of course, eliminate resident apathy and frustration over con-

17. Articles of Incorporation of The Woodlands Community Association, WDC Papers.

18. Interview with Joel Deretchin, February 5, 1982.

19. *Woodlands Villager,* October 16, 1980.

20. Interview with Donald R. Gebert, September 30, 1982; *Woodlands Villager,* July 13, 1977, October 27, 1982.

trol by what some considered a monolithic corporation. One disgruntled resident described the community association as "a caretaker government with no vote for the residents. . . . It's like the fox taking care of the hen house."[21] The company's insistence during the summer of 1978 that a committee formed to help in the administration of a new neighborhood center could be only advisory evoked cries of outrage from aroused residents, who demanded an elected committee with full authority. One citizen exclaimed: "The whole thing is a charade. We can have as many advisory committees as we want but when Mitchell says no, that's it."[22] On the other hand, John Lewis, executive director of The Woodlands Community Association, argued that residents were "listened to more than any other city in the nation." While Lewis's rebuttal may have overstated the case, a compromise decision made three weeks later by the community association to establish a neighborhood center committee composed of elected residents and association-appointed members contradicted the alleged total disregard of resident complaints.[23]

Resident apathy continued, nonetheless, to express itself in various ways—nonattendance at village and community association meetings, low voter turnout for elections to the village and community associations, lack of participation in the resident advisory committee and the wasting away of the pioneer Grogan's Mill Village Association.[24] "We have become," the *Woodlands Villager* editorialized, "a neighborhood of strangers."[25] Persistent resident apathy during the winter of 1979 prompted Jack O'Sullivan to urge his neighbors to become involved in the upcoming election of resident members to the community association. "Don't be fooled," he advised, "by the seeming imbalance of the WCA Board in favor of The Woodlands Development Corporation. The numbers say 'they' will outweigh 'us' by 7 to 3. But the fact that Federal HUD money is involved in The Woodlands gives our three a considerable voice and significantly more power than one might suspect." In closing his plea for citizen involvement, O'Sullivan paid tribute to the company's efforts to ensure that the community association

21. *Woodlands Villager,* June 28, 1978.
22. Ibid., August 2, 1978.
23. Ibid., August 2, 23, 1978.
24. Ibid., August 29, 1979. The literal nonfunctioning of the resident advisory committee system by the spring of 1980 caused Robinson G. Lapp to express "great concern" because the system had been devised to reduce charges of developer control. Minutes of the Board of Directors, The Woodlands Community Association, April 23, 1980.
25. *Woodlands Villager,* April 27, 1977.

did not represent only company goals. "The developer," he assured his fellows, "has recognized the need to provide responsible, citizen-oriented guidance . . . and has appointed many people-minded individuals to the [WCA] board."

Two years later another resident expressed similar sentiments following the company's announcement of plans to transfer management of The Woodlands Athletic Center from the community association to a company subsidiary in order to absorb the center's deficit and to expand its facilities over a two-year period at a cost of $1.5 million. "Any way you look at it," the resident declared, "the WDC and Mitchell Energy . . . have bent over backwards to show their willingness to go a step beyond in making The Woodlands a real fine hometown."[26]

Dissatisfaction with corporate domination of The Woodlands Community Association peaked in the summer of 1981 with the formation of a resident committee by the Panther Creek Village Association to investigate incorporation or annexation by Houston. This action represented little more than wishful thinking since incorporation could be achieved only with Houston's permission, an unlikely event. It was even less likely that Houston would be willing to annex The Woodlands so soon after the controversial annexation of Clear Lake City. Also, interviews conducted at random by the *Woodlands Villager* indicated an ambivalence among residents which led the newspaper's editor to observe: "Incorporation will take a mobilization of the entire community toward a common goal, something yet to be achieved in our new hometown. If the residents of The Woodlands want to be self-governing, they'll have to work for it . . . not just give it lip service."[27] The newspaper later reported that a poll of residents revealed that "few, if any, understand what it [incorporation] is all about."[28] One resident who opposed incorporation observed, "Right now, George Mitchell controls the land situation, and if we want him to keep developing The Woodlands, he needs control." A few months later an attempt by a delegation of residents to prevent the construction of the service station in The Woodlands elicited additional expressions of citizen support for The Woodlands Development Corporation. The furor over the proposed facility, one resident asserted, stemmed from "a small, but noisy group of people. . . . The total effect of the bits and pieces of their attack has been to paint The Woodlands Development Corporation as the enemy of

26. Ibid., January 23, 1979, March 4, 1981.
27. Ibid., July 22, 1981.
28. Ibid., July 29, 1981.

The Reverend Donald R. Gebert addressing a meeting of The Woodlands Community Association.

its own standards of environmental integrity; an injustice to all those men and women who have worked hard and well to bring us this new town which is so beautiful and liveable."[29]

In the midst of these events, and as The Woodlands' population expanded, Interfaith found it necessary to alter its earlier refusal to assume responsibility for the establishment of human-service facilities. The decision to change grew out of its increasing status among residents as a place where they could go for help and an awareness that a critical social-agency gap existed in The Woodlands. Crimes, particularly juvenile-related offenses, and family-oriented behavioral prob-

29. Ibid., July 22, November 11, 1981.

Robinson G. Lapp leading a meeting of The Woodlands Community Association.

lems, while never epidemic, occurred with enough regularity to cause alarmed citizens to ask for remedial action.[30]

Interfaith began its operations in the spring of 1975, using unoccupied space in the Information Center provided by The Woodlands Development Corporation. Its visibility increased throughout the community because of Gebert's activism, a visitation program in which

30. The *Woodlands Villager* regularly reported crime statistics. One police officer reported that major teenage offenses included drugs, theft, and extortion of younger children. He also contended that "The Woodlands has become a mecca for rapists and child molesters because of the pathways of bike trails and the preservation of underbrush." *Woodlands Villager*, July 20, 1977. Robinson Lapp quickly refuted the police officer's description and argued that per capita occurrence of criminal offenses was not extraordinary. *Woodlands Villager*, August 3, 1977.

137

Joel Deretchin preparing for a meeting of The Woodlands Community Association.

representatives of Interfaith visited every newcomer, and compilation of a resident directory, first published in October, 1975. Interfaith's greater visibility soon brought a staggering workload and demands on its limited space. It also became increasingly well known as the "community advocate" to whom people with problems could turn. Early in 1976 a group of mothers appealed to Interfaith for help in establishing a child day-care service, which the developer had promised but which had not materialized. After completing plans for a two-day-a-week drop-in center staffed by volunteers, Interfaith persuaded The Woodlands Development Corporation to provide free space in The Wharf Shopping Mall with the proviso that the residents would fund and conduct the program. From that small beginning by the fall of 1976 The Woodlands Child Development Center had expanded into a five-

138

day-a-week program. In 1977 it moved to new quarters in the recently completed Baptist church, where it offered comprehensive twelve-hour-a-day services.[31]

As the population of The Woodlands grew—from 643 people in 1975 to 3,826 in 1977 and to almost 6,000 by the end of 1978—Interfaith's activities increased apace. Programs it either started independently or helped establish included Boy Scout troops, chapters of Alcoholics Anonymous and Overeaters Anonymous, a Teen Council, a Crisis Action Line to help persons suffering emotional crises, and The Woodlands Resident Aid Program to help the needy and the elderly.[32]

By early 1979, Interfaith had clearly outgrown its quarters, a growth which coincided with residents' increasing interest in building their own center—as Gebert expresses it, "a people's place . . . independent from The Woodlands Development Corporation."[33] In late January, 1979, The Woodlands Development Corporation donated one acre in Panther Creek Village for the construction of the Interfaith Human Services Center, and a group of residents launched a campaign to sell $325,000 in Interfaith bonds. Sale of the bonds proceeded rapidly, and on May 2, 1979, construction of the center began.[34]

After occupying its new quarters in September, 1979, Interfaith's programs continued to expand, as did its reputation as the "community advocate." Its staff, full and part time, grew to 50, with more than 400 vounteers, and included a director of family services, a senior citizens' advocate, and the director of the child-care center. Relations with The Woodlands Development Corporation improved noticeably, a development Gebert attributes to Robinson G. Lapp, director of community operations, and Edward P. Lee, who became president of the corporation in November, 1977. After the company donated more land to Interfaith in July, 1981, Gebert publicly praised the corporation's cooperative spirit, generosity, and selflessness in its relations not only with Interfaith but also with the entire community. The corporation, Gebert stated, "has continued to enable us to serve the community as it grows. In fact, the WDC is very supportive of all non-profit institutions that are serving the people of The Woodlands and . . . without ever interfering with the operational process of the institutions."[35]

In retrospect, The Woodlands Development Corporation's difficul-

31. Franzmeier and Gebert, Woodlands Experience, pp. 25–26, 52–53.
32. Ibid., pp. 50, 55–60.
33. Interview with Donald R. Gebert, September 30, 1982.
34. Woodlands Villager, January 31, May 2, 1979.
35. Interview with Donald R. Gebert, September 30, 1982; Woodlands Villager, July 29, 1981.

ties in relation to institutional development during the period 1975 through 1977 stemmed not from corporate arrogance, aloofness, or lack of commitment, as some residents and others charged, but from internal organizational confusion and a consequent lapse in communications, which heightened existing tensions. Most of all, the economic recession, the failure of federal funding to materialize, internal financial crisis, and inadequate population and employment bases in The Woodlands combined to distract attention from social goals and rendered their attainment impractical and even impossible.

George Mitchell invested considerable time, money, and effort in social planning until the summer of 1974, when mounting financial troubles subordinated social goals to survival. His renewed efforts following financial recovery to realize at least some of those goals are evidence that he never abandoned his original intentions.

It is also true that in The Woodlands, as in most other communities, recognition by its residents of shared problems and awareness of the need for united action to find solutions provided the most effective forces for the formation of a sense of community. In The Woodlands, unlike most other communities, the presence of the corporation, regardless of how muted its voice or benevolent its posture, and the peculiar town governance provided for in the project agreement made the identification of local leadership more difficult, though not impossible. In fact, The Woodlands Community Association and especially the village associations formed by the residents provided forums for potential community leaders, the airing of grievances, and discussion of community-wide concerns. Thus within its only internal political outlets the community produced its own leaders, including Jack O'Sullivan, Randy Hanselka, George Anyedi, Dick Beer, Jack Felton, John Standish, Steve Schoonover, and Muriel Moore. Population growth made possible the establishment of permanent religious organizations, housed in independently owned facilities. Those institutions, their congregations, and the clergymen heading them augmented the community-service functions provided by Interfaith and Donald R. Gebert and, most of all, further cemented the bonds of community.

Other elements that contributed to a community esprit de corps included the *Woodlands Villager* and its editor-publisher, David Slavin, who over the years repeatedly editorialized and at times harangued on the subject of community-mindedness; and a number of resident-founded civic organizations, such as The Woodlands Living Arts Council, The Woodlands Community Theatre, and the Rotary, Lions, and Optimist clubs, provided outlets and programs for participatory community development.

140

Most important, as communalization proceeded, residents in The Woodlands increasingly turned away from their initial predilection to seek redress of grievances through petition to the corporation and, failing there, to HUD and began solving problems for themselves. Thus when idle, bored teenagers in the community became an apparent disruptive force, residents met to allow the youngsters an opportunity to air their views and to seek remedies. When traffic problems, particularly speeding motorists, unregulated intersections, and inadequate access roads to and from I-45, demanded remedial action, residents began exerting pressure on county officials and formed a living petition to wring approval from the state highway commission for improved interstate highway interchanges. When the always underfunded Woodlands Community Association found itself unable to maintain the neighborhood parks and centers, residents formed volunteer work teams who spent weekends and working days laboring in the neighborhood recreational areas.

At the same time The Woodlands Community Association also enlarged its role in the new town. Because it depended for its income on assessments levied on property owners, the association found itself unable to fulfill its intended functions during the early years when the population was low. Continued underfunding brought the association to its nadir in the summer of 1979 with the announcement by Executive Director Donald Rieke that vandalism and lack of maintenance had reduced neighborhood parks and many recreational centers throughout The Woodlands to a state of disrepair. Other services provided by the association equally suffered from the organization's insufficient funding until the population began to mushroom in the 1980s. In the interim the association at least served notice of its potential as a viable community-service organization when in November, 1981, after nearly three years of litigation, it won its first legal suit against a resident for violations of the association's covenants. During the same year the association achieved financial vitality that allowed budget allocations of nearly $4 million and expanded responsibilities.[36]

In this fashion a community began to form in The Woodlands, finding its impetus in diverse sources. George Mitchell and The Woodlands Development Corporation contributed to its growth both overtly and implicitly, but never unilaterally. In the process both the company and the people profited.

36. This summary of community development was taken from articles and editorials in the *Woodlands Villager,* the *Conroe Daily Courier,* and Minutes of the Board of Directors, The Woodlands Community Association.

9. Epilogue

The end of the year 1975 marked the low point in the fortunes of The Woodlands Development Corporation and The Woodlands. Population, completed dwelling units, and the number of industrial and business firms locating in the project lagged far behind the optimistic projections of 1971–72. Social services consisted of a three-man police force provided by Montgomery County and paid for by The Woodlands Community Association, two schools (one elementary and one intermediate), and an eight-man fire department. Missing were medical facilities, an internal transit system, a wide range of human-service and cultural facilities, and a university campus.

Assets enjoyed by The Woodlands, on the other hand, included a remarkable amenities system and an environmental design which led HUD to describe the project as "the most environmentally responsible and innovative of all the new communities."[1] The environmental achievements were largely due to the success of The Woodlands' plan-

---

1. Arthur B. Shostak, "Technological Innovation in the American New Communities," in Gideon Golany, ed., *Innovations for Future Cities,* p. 8. In a 1980 survey conducted by a management consulting firm involving 270 residents of The Woodlands, over 90 percent indicated strong satisfaction with overall conditions. The residents expressed particular satisfaction with the concept, natural setting, and recreational facilities. The greatest dissatisfactions noted were the distance from Houston and malfunctioning streetlights. The most-needed service additions mentioned included medical facilities, a public transportation system, and a dogcatcher. Mel DuPaix to Edward P. Lee and Roger Galatas, September 30, 1980, WDC Papers.

ners in applying the theories of Ian McHarg. But even this most laud-
able achievement of the new town had its critics. Some environmentalists complained that too much of the woods had been razed to accommodate golf courses, and they railed against McHarg's network of
paths, which had been laid in concrete instead of wood chips. McHarg
sagely pointed out that "it would be very nice if the forest remained
a forest, but if it remained a forest it would not be a new town." He
did, however, join the critics in their dislike of the concrete paths, which
he described as "incredibly expensive and entirely inappropriate." Always loath to let slip an opportunity to offer a barbed comment, McHarg
added that in his opinion the major strength of his environmental design was that "builders found . . . they could love money and trees at
the same time."[2]

Money—that is, the financial resources of the Mitchell Energy and
Development Corporation—was, of course, another asset and the most
vital prerequisite of The Woodlands' success. One by one the other
Title VII new communities failed, brought down by low residential sales,
inability to attract industry, expensive infrastructure, high overhead, and
lack of federal subsidies. The Woodlands confronted the same problems but managed to persist primarily because of the parent company's
financial strength. A major additional asset was the presence at the
company's helm of George Mitchell, who never wavered in his conviction that, given time, the new town, because of its location and the
advantages it offered, would progress from annual deficits to profits.[3]

Another source of strength enjoyed by The Woodlands was Mitchell's success, after some false starts, in putting together an experienced
and sensitive management team. Edward P. Lee, president of The Woodlands Development Corporation from November, 1977, until his death
in June, 1986, had previously served as vice-president of land development operations at Irvine, California, considered by some to be the
most successful new town in the United States. After graduating from
Saint Edward's University, in Austin, Texas, Lee earned a master's degree from the University of Notre Dame and a master's degree in business administration with a concentration in urban land analysis from
the University of California at Los Angeles. Lee was a businessman with

2. *Washington Post,* January 12, 1975.
3. Mitchell commented in January, 1977: "It is apparent that some investors have
been uneasy about the Company's involvement [in The Woodlands]; now, however, there
seems to be a trend towards perceiving our holdings as an under-valued asset. . . . Residential, commercial, industrial and retail population of The Woodlands is fast reaching
that point of critical mass where more begets more." Mitchell Energy and Development
Corporation, Annual Report, Year Ended January 31, 1977, p. 3.

an eye on the profit column, but he also possessed, in Donald Gebert's words, "an excellent personal value system," which contributed to improved relations with residents of The Woodlands. After assuming the post as head of The Woodlands Development Corporation, Lee took the lead in developing three- and five-year operating plans and introduced a "profit center" organizational structure, both of which minimized wasted capital and facilitated orderly development. Lee also caught new-town fever and emphatically asserted that "The Woodlands is going to be a state of the art new town . . . a world-class development."[4] Robinson G. Lapp, an ordained minister of the United Church of Christ, a former member of the new-town staff at Gananda, New York, and a former executive director of the Metro Denver Fair Housing Center, brought tact, efficiency, organizational skill, and sensitivity to his dual role as director of government relations and director of community operations.[5] Lapp's successor, Joel Deretchin, a ten-year veteran of the new-community program, shares Lapp's qualities, especially his awareness of human needs.[6] Richard P. Browne, one of the few remaining members of the original planning team and senior vice-president of community planning and development, continues to be a totally committed advocate of the new-town experiment. Sometimes referred to as "the conscience of The Woodlands," he is near evangelistic in his conviction that America can build cities that harmonize the individual, community, and nature.[7]

Financial success came slowly but steadily to The Woodlands Development Corporation. Residential dwellings completed through September, 1976, numbered 548, and population had reached 1,774.[8] By mid-July, 1980, the population of The Woodlands had leaped to 8,800 persons living in 2,951 households, and 170 business and industrial firms employing 3,000 people had located in the new town, which now boasted 6 public schools and 12 churches.[9] The year 1980

4. *Conroe Daily Courier,* November 29, 1977; interview with Donald R. Gebert, September 30, 1982; interview with Edward P. Lee, February 5, 1982; *Houston Post,* June 25, 1986.

5. *Woodlands Villager,* January 31, 1979, April 8, 1981; interview with Robinson G. Lapp, February 23, 1981.

6. *Woodlands Villager,* May 13, 1981; interview with Joel Deretchin, February 5, 1982.

7. Jan Short, "Home to The Woodlands," *Houston City Magazine* 7 (January, 1983): 78; interview with Richard P. Browne, August 6, 1980.

8. *Grogan's Mill Villager,* October 16, 1976. Mitchell Energy and Development Corporation, Annual Report, Year Ended January 31, 1977, p. 21, sets the population at year's end at almost two thousand.

9. *Woodlands Villager,* July 16, 1980.

also brought an all-time high of 685 new-home sales and an increase of population by year's end to 10,000, plus a total of 200 business and industrial firms providing over 4,000 jobs.[10]

Continued expansion during 1981 led Mitchell to comment that "The Woodlands is rapidly becoming one of the 'hottest' real estate undertakings in the United States." New-home sales for the year totaled 865, occupied dwellings rose to 4,866, and the number of residents increased to 13,640. Development began on Cochran's Crossing Village, the third of six planned villages. Additional advances included a total of 231 business and industrial firms employing 4,980 persons, a record sale of 705 lots, and the completion and leasing of six office, commercial, and industrial buildings.[11] These figures are impressive, though they failed to meet the 1972 projections of 10,751 completed residential units, including 2,342 for low- and moderate-income families, and a population of 34,697 through 1981.[12]

Other events of 1980–81 not as clearly associated with profit-and-loss columns signaled the establishment of long-postponed social institutions in The Woodlands. In the spring of 1980, after more than two years of planning and one rejection by the Houston-Galveston Area Council, The Woodlands Medical Center, Inc., a nonprofit organization, received approval to build a family health center in The Woodlands.[13] Groundbreaking for the facility on June 24, 1981, coincided with an announcement by The Woodlands Medical Center, Inc., and the Montgomery County Hospital District Board of Directors of an agreement providing for construction of a ninety-six-bed general hospital in The Woodlands. Approval of the plan by the Texas Health Facilities Commission in late 1981, and its opening in January, 1985, meant that a medical-care system, though nearly a decade behind original schedules and in no way futuristic, had begun to develop in the new town.[14]

During 1981, Mitchell also began a campaign to establish the Houston area as a major regional research-and-development center. For that purpose Mitchell invited the University of Houston, Texas A&M University, the University of Texas at Austin, and Rice University to form a consortium to be known as the Houston Area Research Center. Mitchell Energy and Development Corporation donated a 100-acre

10. Ibid., February 25, 1981.

11. Mitchell Energy and Development Corporation, Annual Report, Year Ended January 31, 1982, pp. 2, 23, 35, 37.

12. Development Plan, schedule 8, p. 10, schedule 12(c), p. 16.

13. Woodlands Villager, April 30, 1980.

14. Ibid., June 24, 1981; Mitchell Energy and Development Corporation, Annual Report, Year Ended January 31, 1982, p. 25.

tract in The Woodlands to house the center, and the company and George Mitchell and his wife, Cynthia, agreed to provide $3.6 million as seed money.[15] In December, 1981, Mitchell Energy and Development Corporation and George and Cynthia Mitchell offered 150 acres and $5.6 million to Texas Medical Center, Inc., for the establishment of a medical-research center in The Woodlands. On the occasion of formally accepting the donations, Philip G. Hoffman, president of Texas Medical Center, Inc., and former president of the University of Houston, stated that facilities would be built in The Woodlands to provide quarters for research and academic programs "at the cutting edge of medical and biomedical sciences." He also predicted that, once operative, the programs would support "exciting work to benefit all mankind."[16]

With rising residential sales and population figures in The Woodlands, plus its investments in ancillary enterprises, The Woodlands Development Corporation earned its first operating profit during 1978.[17] The improving financial status of the company led Mitchell to reiterate confidently an original goal of the new town. "We intend," Mitchell stated in late 1978, "to transplant the entire cross-section of the Houston population into The Woodlands." He hedged his statement with the additional observation that attaining the desired socioeconomic mix depended on obtaining federal subsidies and would take another ten years, but, he asserted, "once our job base explodes, then we can have the cross-section we're trying for."[18]

The available data and current political events qualify somewhat, if they do not contradict, Mitchell's optimism. In terms of attempts to

15. Mitchell Energy and Development Corporation, Annual Report, Year Ended January 31, 1982, p. 2, 23; Woodlands Villager, November 11, 1981, February 3, 1982.

16. Mitchell Energy and Development Corporation, Annual Report, Year Ended January 31, 1982, pp. 2, 25; Houston Post, March 25, 1982. An Epidemiology Center became the first component in September, 1982. Woodlands Villager, September 8, 1982.

17. Woodlands Villager, December 20, 1978. Operating profit is the figure before interest, general and administrative expenses, and income taxes are calculated. The company's finances were also improved by the receipt of more federal grants and payments by municipal utility districts in The Woodlands for water, sewer, and drainage systems. Through 1979, The Woodlands Development Corporation received a total of $16 million in direct federal grants. The community benefited from an additional $8.8 million in grants for improvement of amenities, wastewater treatment facilities, and a branch library. At that time the company also received a total of $17.4 million in payments from the municipal utility districts. Mitchell Energy and Development Corporation, Annual Report, Year Ended January 31, 1980, pp. 23, 27. On the other hand, Mitchell Energy and Development Corporation had invested more than $200 million in the new-town project through the summer of 1982. Houston Post, August 4, 1982.

18. Woodlands Villager, November 29, 1978.

Edward P. Lee, president, Woodlands Development Corporation (front right), *with fellow executives Vernon Robbins* (front left) *and* (back, left to right) *Edward Dreiss and J. Leonard Rogers.*

attract an economic and ethnic mix, The Woodlands has achieved its best record in providing rent-assisted apartment units for the elderly and for low-income families. By the end of 1982, of a total 1,679 such residents, 902, or 53.7 percent, were receiving rent assistance. Efforts to attract ethnic minorities have fared less well: as of December 31, 1982, the total population in the new town had reached 16,009, with 1,418, or 8.8 percent, in minority categories.[19] Median prices for homes in The Woodlands, ranging from $42,000 in 1975 to $77,600 in 1982, reinforce its image as a middle- and upper-income community, as does

19. "The Woodlands–Cumulative Apartments, 1974–1985," WDC Papers; "Ethnicity of The Woodlands Population as of December, 1982," WDC Papers.

George and Cynthia Mitchell and Ian and Carol McHarg at The Woodlands' tenth anniversary celebration, October 20, 1984.

the high median income of its residents. The election of President Ronald Reagan in 1980 and the advent of so-called supply-side economics lessened, if they did not preclude, the chances of obtaining federal subsidies. The priority given to urban development by a chief executive who greeted his secretary of housing and urban development at a White House reception with the salutation "Hello, Mr. Mayor" speaks for itself, as does the phasing out of HUD's Office of New Community Development.[20]

In August, 1982, HUD announced that it was negotiating with The

20. Short, "Home to The Woodlands," p. 77; memorandum, Mel DuPaix to Charles Simpson, August 8, 1983, WDC Papers; *Wall Street Journal,* January 7, 1983; "Trivia Quiz on 1982," *Newsweek* 100 (December 27, 1982): 37; *Houston Post,* August 4, 1982. In

Woodlands Development Corporation for a severance of the project agreement. The Termination Agreement, signed by representatives of HUD and of The Woodlands Commercial Development Company (successor to The Woodlands Development Corporation and presently known as The Woodlands Corporation) on April 21, 1983, formally released The Woodlands from its status as a Title VII new town.[21] The agreement also stipulates that the developer will comply with modified affirmative action and plans for low-to-moderate-income housing incorporated as parts of the new document. In both plans the developer is expected to use "best efforts" to attain minority and low-to-moderate-income population mixes, but in neither case are penalties established in the event the desired population percentages are not achieved.[22]

While The Woodlands will go on to completion and while many of the social goals embodied in the 1970 legislation will continue to be sought, termination of the uneasy partnership with HUD ends an era in the development of the new town. The exact path that The Woodlands will follow in the future depends on many variables and most of all on the ability of George Mitchell to balance visionary ideals with the hard realities of the marketplace. In view of his past record, which clearly attests to the totality of his commitment to all of the new-community program's objectives, it is likely that he will continue to commit his personal financial resources and those of his company to attainment of these goals. Several planned and ongoing projects in

---

December, 1982, Reagan further demonstrated the priority given to urban problems by announcing his intention to freeze $465 million in unexpected urban funds from fiscal 1982. *Houston Post,* December 31, 1982.

21. *Houston Post,* August 4, 1982; Termination Agreement, April 21, 1983, WDC Papers. The interest of the government is secured by an indenture of mortgage and deed of trust and by an irrevocable letter of credit. Also, the developer is required to pay an annual fee equal to 1 percent of the principal amount of outstanding debentures.

22. Termination Agreement, April 21, 1983. The Affirmative Action plan requires the developer to seek to attract minorities to The Woodlands and establishes desired minority percentages as follows: 8 percent of a total population of 20,000; 9 percent of a total population of 40,000; 11 percent of a total population of 60,000; 13.5 percent of a total population of 80,000; and 15 percent of a total population of 100,000. Upon completion of the project the population would reflect the minority mix in the Houston SMSA. The low-to-moderate-income housing plan requires the developer to use "best efforts" to cause subsidized housing units, both rental (section 235) and sale (section 8), to be started each year equaling 15 percent of the average annual number of all units started during the preceding three years. In years in which federal funds are not available, the developer is released from any responsibility. As of November 30, 1984, the population of The Woodlands had reached 18,733, with a total minority representation of 8.8 percent. Interview with Mel DuPaix, January 9, 1985.

The Woodlands augur well for the future. Construction of the third residential village, Cochran's Crossing, began in late summer, 1982, aided by a $2 million community block grant from HUD for infrastructure. Completion during 1986 of a new access road and bridge across Spring Creek was anticipated, as movement between all the villages in The Woodlands and Houston's northwest suburbs would be facilitated.[23] Development of a seventy-five-acre regional shopping mall to be completed in spring, 1987, as a joint venture with Homart Development Company, a Sears, Roebuck and Company subsidiary, promises accelerated economic growth and expanded employment opportunities, as does construction in the Research Forest, the site of facilities housing the Houston Area Research Center; the Texas Medical Center, Inc.; and private-enterprise high-technology centers.[24] Contracts have been agreed to by Methodist Hospital Health Care System, Inc., to operate the ninety-six-bed community hospital completed in early 1985, and further additions to the work force have resulted from expansion by firms already in The Woodlands as well as the entry of new enterprises.[25]

Without question Mitchell's perseverance in the face of a host of economic, administrative, and political problems largely beyond his power to control allowed The Woodlands, alone among the Title VII new towns, not only to live but to grow. Given time, a favorable economic climate, and enlightened, responsible leadership, The Woodlands may yet prove to be an object lesson to the American people on how best to order their lives in the place most must call home — the American city.

23. *Houston Post,* August 8, 1982; Mitchell Energy and Development Corporation, Annual Report, Year Ended January 31, 1983, p. 20.

24. Mitchell Energy and Development Corporation, Annual Report, Year Ended January 31, 1983, p. 20.

25. *Houston Post,* September 18, 1983; Mitchell Energy and Development Corporation, Annual Report, Year Ended January 31, 1983, pp. 20–21.

Bibliography

Corporate Records

Gladstone Associates. Development Program, Mitchell-Houston New Community. Baltimore, Md., August, 1971.

——. Market Opportunities, Mitchell-Houston New Community. Baltimore, Md., March, 1971.

——. Metropolitan Economic Background, Mitchell-Houston New Community. Baltimore, Md., March, 1971.

The McAlister Company. Reading File, New Town Project. Houston.

Mitchell Energy and Development Corporation. Annual Reports. 1968–85.

Turner, Collie and Braden, Inc. A Case History of The Woodlands – A Project of The Woodlands Development Corporation: Land Development Engineering for a "New Town." Houston, 1972.

Wallace, McHarg, Roberts and Todd. Woodlands New Community: An Ecological Plan. Report prepared for The Woodlands Development Corporation. May, 1974.

Woodlands Community Association. Articles of Incorporation.

——. Minutes of the Board of Directors. 1976–81.

Woodlands Development Corporation [WDC]. Indenture of Mortgage and Deed of Trust, The Woodlands Development Corporation to the Chase Manhattan Bank, Trustee. August 23, 1972.

——. Papers. The Woodlands Tex. Letters, manuscripts, memoranda, internal reports, press releases, unpublished chronicles. 1968–85.

——. Termination Agreement. April 21, 1983.

151

Public Documents

Booz-Allen and Hamilton, Inc. *New Communities: Problems and Potentials.* Appendix C: "An Assessment of the Causes of Current Problems, Case Study H: Woodlands." Washington, D.C., 1976.

Congressional Record. 90th Cong., 2nd sess. (1968).

———. 91st Cong., 2nd sess. (1970).

Leventhal, Kenneth, and Company. *Report on Intensive Studies of Selected New Community Projects.* Washington, D.C., 1978.

State of the Union Message, President Richard M. Nixon, January 20, 1970. H. Doc. 91–266. 91st Cong., 2nd sess.

U.S. Congress. House. *Housing and Urban Development Legislation and Urban Insurance: Hearings before a Subcommittee on Housing of the Committee on Banking and Currency.* 90th Cong., 2nd sess. (1968).

———. *Oversight Hearings on HUD New Communities Program: Hearings before a Subcommittee on Housing of the Committee on Banking and Currency.* 93rd Cong., 1st sess. (1973).

———. Senate. *Housing and Urban Development Act.* S. Rep. 1123. 90th Cong., 2nd sess. (1968).

U.S. Statutes at Large. 84:1791–1805.

Vernon's Texas Codes Annotated. 1972. II, 274–344, 542–620.

Newspapers

Boston Sunday Globe. 1975, 1977.
Central Maryland News. 1971.
Conroe Daily Courier. 1972–78.
Galveston Daily News. 1974.
Grogan's Mill Villager. 1976.
Houston Business Journal. 1976.
Houston Chronicle. 1973–77.
Houston Post. 1971–86.
Texas Builder. 1974.
Wall Street Journal. 1983.
Washington Post. 1975.
Woodlands Newsletter. 1973–74.
Woodlands Sun. 1974, 1976.
Woodlands Villager. 1977–83.

Interviews

Richard P. Browne, August 6, 1980.
Joel Deretchin, February 5, 1982.

Mel DuPaix, January 9, 1985.
Donald R. Gebert, September 30, 1982.
Charles Kelly, August 31, 1982.
Robinson G. Lapp, February 23, 1981.
Edward P. Lee, February 5, 1982; October 31, 1984.
Charles Lively, August 5, 6, 1980.
George P. Mitchell, October 16, 1977.
J. Leonard Rogers, October 31, 1984.
Coulson Tough, August 31, 1982.
Randall Woods, October 31, 1984.

Books and Periodicals

Allen, Gerald. "A Last Word—New Towns: Re-Creation Not Transformation." *Architectural Record* 154 (December, 1973): 142–44.

Arnold, Joseph L. *The New Deal in the Suburbs: A History of the Greenbelt Town Program, 1936–1954.* Columbus: Ohio State University Press, 1971.

Barnett, Jonathan. "How Are 'Planned Communities' Planned? Designing New Communities." *Architectural Record* 154 (December, 1973): 120–29.

Breckenfeld, Gurney. *Columbia and the New Cities.* New York: Ives Washburn, 1971.

Brooks, Richard O. *New Towns and Communal Values: A Case Study of Columbia, Maryland.* New York: Praeger Publishers, 1974.

Campbell, Carlos C. *New Towns: Another Way to Live.* Reston, Va.: Reston Publishing Co., 1976.

"Can 'New Towns' Survive the Economic Crunch?" *Business Week* 2367 (February 10, 1975): 43–44.

Clapp, James A. *New Towns and Urban Policy: Planning Metropolitan Growth.* New York: Dunellen Publishing Co., 1971.

Conkin, Paul K. *Tomorrow a New World: The New Deal Community Program.* Ithaca, N.Y.: Cornell University Press, 1959.

Curtis, Tom. "Masterbuilder George Mitchell Is No Ordinary Oilman." *Sky,* September, 1977, pp. 41–78.

Davies, Richard O. *The Age of Asphalt: The Automobile, the Freeway, and the Condition of Metropolitan America.* Philadelphia, New York, and Toronto: J. B. Lippincott Co., 1975.

Farley, Dennis. "Land Politics: Ian McHarg." *Atlantic Monthly* 233 (January, 1974): 10–17.

Franzmeier, Alvin H., and Donald R. Gebert. *The Woodlands Experience: An Unfinished History of the Interfaith Movement in a New*

Town in Texas. The Woodlands, Tex.: The Woodlands Religious Community, 1979.

Gimlin, Hoyt. "New Towns." In William B. Dickinson, Jr., ed., *Editorial Research Reports on the Urban Environment.* Washington, D.C.: Congressional Quarterly, 1969.

Griffith, Robert. "Truman and the Historians." *Wisconsin Magazine of History* 59 (Autumn, 1975): 20–47.

Hofstadter, Richard. *The Age of Reform: From Bryan to F.D.R.* New York: Alfred A. Knopf, 1955.

Jacobs, Scott. "New Towns – or Ghost Towns?" *Planning* 41 (January, 1975): 15–18.

Johnson, Lyndon B. *Message on Cities – Message from the President of the United States.* H. Doc. 99. Reprinted in Milton Speizman, ed., *Urban America in the Twentieth Century.* New York: Thomas Y. Crowell Co., 1968.

Karp, Richard. "Building Chaos: The New Town Program Is Multimillion-Dollar Mess." *Barron's National Business and Financial Weekly* 56 (September 6, 1976): 3–12.

Kassler, Elizabeth. "New Towns, New Cities." In *The New City: Architecture and Urban Renewal.* New York: Museum of Modern Art, 1967.

Laurence, John W. "Address to the Board of Directors, Urban America, Inc.," New Orleans, La., May 16, 1966. Reprinted in Milton Speizman, ed., *Urban America in the Twentieth Century.* New York: Thomas Y. Crowell, 1968.

Link, Arthur S., and William B. Catton. *American Epoch: A History of the United States since the 1890s.* 3 vols. New York: Alfred A. Knopf, 1967.

Lubove, Roy. "The Roots of Urban Planning." In Allen M. Wakstein, ed., *The Urbanization of America: An Historical Anthology.* Boston and New York: Houghton Mifflin, 1970.

McCahill, Ed. "Soul City – More Than a Pea Patch." *Planning* 41 (August, 1975): 20–21.

McFarland, M. Carter. *Federal Government and Urban Problems: HUD – Successes, Failures, and the Fate of Our Cities.* Boulder, Colo.: Westview Press, 1978.

McHarg, Ian. *Design with Nature.* Garden City, N.Y.: Natural History Press, 1969.

McHarg, Ian, and Jonathan Sutton. "Ecological Plumbing for the Texas Coastal Plain: The Woodlands New Town Experiment." *Landscape Architecture* 65 (January, 1975): 78–89.

Mayer, Martin. *The Builders: Houses, People, Neighborhoods, Government, Money.* New York: W. W. Norton, 1978.

Nash, Roderick. *Wilderness and the American Mind.* New Haven, Conn., and London: Yale University Press, 1967.

"New Towns That Haunt HUD." *Business Week* 2427 (April 12, 1976): 36.

"Nobody's Laughing Now." *Forbes Magazine* 127 (March 2, 1981): 84–88.

"Picking Up the Pieces of HUD's New Towns." *Business Week* 2446 (August 23, 1976): 30.

"Privately Financed New Communities." *Architectural Record* 154 (December, 1973): 108–19.

"Ready To Roll." *Houston* 31 (September, 1960): 56.

Schmertz, Mildred F. "New Hopes, New Options, but No Money: Whatever Happened to Title VII?" *Architectural Record* 154 (December, 1973): 86–87.

Short, Jan. "Home to The Woodlands." *Houston City Magazine* 7 (January, 1983): 59–63, 77–78.

Shostak, Arthur B. "Technological Innovation in the American New Communities." In Gideon Golany, ed. *Innovations for Future Cities.* New York, Washington, and London: Praeger Publishers, 1976.

Smith, Henry Nash. *Virgin Land: The American West as Symbol and Myth.* Cambridge, Mass.: Harvard University Press, 1950.

Smookler, Helene V. "Administration Hara-Kiri: Implementation of the Urban Growth and New Community Development Act." *Annals of the American Academy of Political and Social Science* 422 (November, 1975): 129–40.

Speizman, Milton, ed. *Urban America in The Twentieth Century.* New York. Thomas Y. Crowell, 1968.

Steiner, Frederick. *The Politics of New Town Planning: The Newfields, Ohio, Story.* Athens: University of Ohio Press, 1981.

"Trivia Quiz on 1982." *Newsweek* 100 (December 27, 1982): 37.

Wantuck, Mary-Margaret. "Those New Towns, 15 Years Later." *Nation's Business* 71 (October, 1983): 42–44.

Warner, Charles A. *Texas Oil and Gas since 1543.* Houston: Gulf Publishing Co., 1939.

Watterson, Wayt T., and Roberta Watterson. *The Politics of New Communities: A Case Study of San Antonio Ranch.* New York: Praeger Publishers, 1975.

Index

157

Reagan, Ronald, 148
recreation centers, 141
"Regional City" synthesis, 12
Regional Planning Association of America, 12, 13
Reid, Kerry Melville, 109
Religious Institutional Planning Committee: formation of, 128
Religious Institutions Planning group, 43
rent assistance, 111, 112, 147
Research Forest, 150
Residential Design Review Committee: environmental control by, 121
Rice University, 114, 145
Riecke, Donald, 141
Riessen, Marty, 109
Rigby, Owens, 45
River Plantation, 23
Robbins, Vernon, 124, 147; flood assessment by, 123
Rogers, J. Leonard, 102, 147; construction by, 115–16; as vice president of WDC, 100–101
Roman Catholic Diocese of Galveston-Houston, 25
Romney, George, 19; departure of, 68; urban reform and, 18, 67
Ross, Cerf, 28, 29, 39
Rotary Club, 140
Rouse, James, 17, 28, 53; professional experiences of, 52; testimony of, 15–16
Rouse Company, 15, 30, 48
Rush, James W., 61
Ryan, William F.: urban planning and, 18
Ryland Homes, 112

Sam Houston State University, 96–98
San Jacinto River, 24
Sanders, Doug: as director of golf, 105–107
Sawmill Community Center, 129–30
Schoonover, Steve, 140
Sears and Burns (law firm), 92
service clubs, 140
Settler's Corner, 110
Shenandoah, 92–94
Shepherd Park Plaza, 23
Simon, Robert, 28

Slavin, David, 140
slums: growth of, 11, 13–15
Smith, Dick A.: as head of Swim Center, 109
Snap-on Tools Corporation, offices for, 112
social planning, 39–43, 140, 149
social services, 142
social unrest, 15
Soil Conservation Service, U.S., 56, 118
South Texas Junior College, 95
Spring Creek, 59, 60, 123, 150
Stack, Robert, 108
Standish, John, 140
Stein, Clarence: urban planning and, 12
Stephens, Robert G., Jr.: urban planning and, 19
Stewart-Woodlands Title Company, Inc., 84
Stolz, Otto G., 83
Superior Oil Company, 112, 113
Sutton-Mann tract: acquisition of, 25–27
Swim Center, 108–109

Tamarac Pines Apartments, 112
Tamina Mill Community Center, 129
Teague, Robert P., Sr.: Woodlands campus and, 97–98
Technology Park, 110–12
Teen Council, 139
Termination Agreement (Woodlands): signing of, 149
Texaco, Inc., 101
Texas A&M University, 4–6, 98, 105, 114, 145
Texas College and University System, 94
Texas Health Facilities Commission, 145
Texas Medical Center, Inc., 115, 146, 150
Texas State Coordinating Board, 40
Thompson, Morris, 41
Timberlake, 123
Timber Ridge, 23, 123
Time and Space (film advertisement), 3
Title I, 86, 88; attack on, 19
Title IV, 18; deletion of, 16
Title VII, 53, 76, 77, 84, 85, 143, 149, 150; passage of, 20
Title X, 28
Tough, Coulson, 39

161

The Woodlands was composed into type on a Compugraphic digital phototypesetter in ten point Optima with two points of spacing between the lines. Helvetica was selected for display. The book was designed by Jim Billingsley, composed by Metricomp, Inc., printed offset by Thomson-Shore Inc., and bound by John H. Dekker & Sons. The paper on which this book is printed bears acid-free characteristics for an effective life of at least three hundred years.

TEXAS A&M UNIVERSITY PRESS : COLLEGE STATION